Remember, no man
is a failure who has
Friends —

Jimmy Stewart

It's a Wonderful Life

Also by Stephen Cox

The Beverly Hillbillies

The Munchkins Remember: The Wizard of Oz and Beyond

The Munsters

The Abbott & Costello Story: 60 Years of Who's On First?
(with John Lofflin)

The Addams Chronicles

The Hooterville Handbook: A Viewer's Guide to Green Acres

Here's Johnny!

Here on Gilligan's Isle
(with Russell Johnson)

The Munchkins of Oz

Cooking in Oz
(with Elaine Willingham)

Dreaming of Jeannie: TV's Prime Time in a Bottle

It's a Wonderful Life

A MEMORY BOOK

STEPHEN COX

Foreword by BOB ANDERSON
("Young George Bailey")

Cumberland House
Nashville, Tennessee

To birth, death, and that wondrous thing in between;

and

for Auld Lang Syne.

Published by
Cumberland House Publishing
431 Harding Industrial Drive
Nashville, Tennessee 37211

About the Cover: Photographer Gaston Longet artfully captured this sobering moment of enlightenment, when George Bailey realizes he's truly lost in a "Twilight Zone."

Broadcast rights to *It's a Wonderful Life* are owned by Republic Entertainment Inc.,® a subsidiary of Spelling Entertainment Group. Republic Entertainment has not approved or endorsed this publication.

Cover design: Unlikely Suburban Design
Text design: Mary Sanford

Library of Congress Cataloging-in-Publication Data
Cox, Stephen, 1966-
  It's a wonderful life : a memory book / Stephen Cox ; foreword by Bob Anderson ("Young George Bailey").
      p. cm.
Includes index.
  ISBN 1-58182-337-1 (alk. paper)
  1. It's a wonderful life (Motion picture) I. Title.
  PN1997.I758C68 2003
  791.43'72'0973--dc22

                                                        2003017050

Printed in Canada
1 2 3 4 5 6 7—09 08 07 06 05 04 03

Contents

Above: Bobbie Anderson as young George
Bailey. *Right:* Bob Anderson today.

Foreword

I was just twelve when it happened, so I really hadn't given much thought to my experiences as an actor in *It's a Wonderful Life* until a few years ago. As a child actor, and part of a family of "movie people" dating back to the silents, the motion picture business has always been, for me, just that—a business. Following my years as a young performer, I went into the navy, started a family, then spent the rest of my career grinding out a living in the production end of film and television until my current semi-retirement.

Decades flew by. Out of the blue, in 1996, as the fiftieth anniversary of *It's a Wonderful Life* approached, I was contacted by Jimmy Hawkins (a personable former child actor himself) who played little Tommy in *Wonderful Life*. He politely tugged on my sleeve saying "s'cuse me," you might say, and asked if I'd be willing to participate in some of the special events celebrating the movie's milestone. I agreed, maybe hesitatingly.

I was blindsided and stunned by the popularity of the film. There were celebrations, movie screenings, parades, personal appearances around the country, and autograph signings— sometimes with thousands of adoring fans who love this old movie.

I was totally unaware how cherished this film had become and is to so many people. Who knew?

I distinctly remember being a little uneasy when my wife, Victoria, and I traveled back east to New York City for an appearance on television at NBC on the *Today* show. I was asked to come out on the street at Rockefeller Center to be interviewed that chilly December morning. When they asked the audience gathered outside, "Do you know who this is?" the people just hummed and stared. My stomach dropped. But when Bryant Gumbel announced, "This is Bobbie Anderson, who portrayed Jimmy Stewart as a child in *It's a Wonderful Life*," the crowd went bananas. I remember men and women holding their young children and older ladies reaching over the fence enclosure, people trying to shake my hand. I stood there and thought, this is just craziness. After we were finished inside the studio and my microphone was removed, I exited the studio's back entrance and there must have been a hundred people out there waiting to get an autograph and take snapshots. It was really funny, and I loved every minute of it.

During a succession of personal appearances over that holiday season, all of the questions posed by the fans and reporters revived memories of my childhood, especially my experiences with Frank Capra, Lionel Barrymore, Thomas Mitchell, and H. B. Warner. I hadn't really thought much about that in decades, and it was nice to know that after slugging it out with the studios as a production guy for more than thirty years, people remembered my on-camera work when I was young, and that they appreciated my performance.

I realize what a monumental motion picture *It's a Wonderful Life* is, and I'm honored to have contributed to such a classic. It's enriched my life tremendously. Now, when I reflect on my career in this insane, dog-eat-dog business, I can truly say (and with thanks to all of the film's devoted admirers) . . . it really was a wonderful life!

"Hee Haw!" And Merry Christmas!

BOB ANDERSON

Acknowledgments

It's true: "Each man's life touches so many other lives." The effect ripples through time, mysterious, unpredictable, nearly incalculable.

We should all be so lucky to have an angel like Clarence to swoop in and fidget and fix. While writing this book, I had many such positive influences, sometimes from people I didn't know from Adam's off ox. But that didn't deter, because they share a love for this film.

Foremost, my thanks to Ron Pitkin at Cumberland House publishing for believing in this book right from the start, and to editor Mary Sanford, talented and unfaltering. I am grateful to the generous people whom I interviewed over the years, those who stood right there in Capra's watchful eye in 1946, probably not realizing they were creating a masterpiece of filmmaking: Jimmy Stewart, Bob Anderson, Karolyn Grimes, Argentina Brunetti, Todd Karns, Adriana Caselotti, Sheldon Leonard, Charles Lane, Nels Nelson, and Virginia Patton Moss.

My heartfelt thanks to the Academy of Motion Picture Arts & Sciences, Victoria Anderson, Buddy Barnett, Jeanine Basinger, Ken Beck, David Bloom, Carol Brady, Chris Brunell, Ben Bushman, Frank

Capra, Willard Carroll, Brian Chanes, Jerry and Blanche Cox, Brian Cox, Ned Comstock, Bernadette and David Dalton, Megan Dalton, Clay Eals, Richard Goodson, Erika Gorder, Jimmy Hawkins, Paul Henning, Peggy Hess, Ramona Christophel Jones, Doug Kline, John Lofflin, Scott Maiko, Kevin Marhanka, Scott Michaels, Carol Coombs Mueller, Pete Petrucci, Phil Potempa, Rutgers University Library, Ray Savage, Victor Scherle, James Scott, Larry Simms, Mary Jo Slater, Chandler Warren, Wesleyan Cinema Archives, USC Cinema-Television Library.

And to Michele, who, I hope, is watching over, keeping me out of trouble.

+‽+ +‽+ +‽+

A portion of the author's royalties is designated to assist Project Angel Food, a nonprofit organization in Los Angeles that provides meals to those suffering with AIDS. (www.angelfood.org)

For information regarding the Jimmy Stewart Museum in his hometown, access the museum's website: www.jimmy.org. To find the Karolyn Grimes "Zuzu" website, visit www.zuzu.net. More information about the Donna Reed Foundation for the Performing Arts can be found at www.donnareed.org.

Introduction

I said, Frank, if you want me to be in a picture about a guy
that wants to kill himself, and an angel comes down named
Clarence, and he can't swim and I save him and . . . well,
I'm your man. When do we start?

≈JIMMY STEWART

When Jimmy Stewart heard about this film Frank Capra was going
to make, his initial impression was that it was "a little nutty." But he
trusted Capra.

So what *is* this movie really about?

It was just after the hell of World War II when, in Hollywood,
California, *It's a Wonderful Life* was born and set free into the world to
sprinkle holiday cheer upon audiences at Christmastime. The year
was 1946, and the studio strategically tempted moviegoers with a
Jimmy Stewart/Donna Reed romance. One look at the film's original
promotional scheme and advertising shows how they amplified the
love story and downplayed the angel. The movie posters and lobby
cards almost all feature a frisky George Bailey lifting up his bride in
the air playfully, and in some cases the couple was shown locked in
a heated embrace. Romance sold movie tickets, and the studios
weren't about to gamble on the strength of a wing-shy angel.

Frank Capra, an Italian movie director who freely dished out heart and soul in his movies, knew the force of this story lay in the actions of an eager, odd little angel who visits an everyman—and he pitched his concept just that way to his lead, Jimmy Stewart, attempting to entice the actor.

And isn't that the crux of the movie? Isn't this a film about an answer to a prayer?

Over time, the film has traveled an unlikely route, ultimately becoming an American tradition, representing a lot of things to literally untold millions of people around the world. Some are drawn to the wholesome values the film embodies. Others point to this traditional tale's demonstration of the true meaning of Christmas. Still others maintain that it's a film about love of family. It's certainly a manual on solid friendship. Maybe Capra's moral, that every life is precious, sells it best. To be fair, there's no definitive theme to sum

The personal and on-camera chemistry between Jimmy Stewart and Donna Reed was intrinsic for both. Stewart said years later, "I fell in love with her right off the bat . . . I can't put my finger on a time when we ever rehearsed."

USC CINEMA-TELEVISION LIBRARY

up this complex story. It would be pointless to try and single out a most effective motif.

The element *I* like best in *It's a Wonderful Life* is the supernatural one, straight from the heavens, with heroes and miracles. That and the reinforcement of faith. It's not about the tinsel on the tree, or lassoing the moon, gift-wrapped presents, or pocketed rose petals. To me, it's the story of an angel helping a desperate human being.

Clearly, something rescued this film from oblivion forty years after it was made and blessed it with new life and respect. The rebirth of this motion picture itself is nothing short of miraculous. Then again, I believe in angels.

You'll probably think I'm crazy, but I discovered an angel one evening while driving my car, just exiting the busy freeway. A friend and I were heading down the off-ramp and I spotted a homeless man ahead, at the bottom of the hill. Normally, but not always, I try to help the homeless. For some reason, this time I didn't hesitate and grabbed some change from the little pocket area on my dashboard. When I rolled down my window my friend asked, "Are you gonna give that guy money?"

All I thought to answer from the corner of my mouth was "Yeah, it always comes back to you." I had no idea how soon I'd be proven right.

This poor stranger approached as the light turned green, and I quickly handed him the coins. He thanked me and I rolled up the window. Just then, a reckless SUV blasted through the intersection at full speed. There was no way I would have seen it coming. Those few extra seconds had saved our lives. My entire body broke out in a cold sweat and I had to pull over to absorb the fact that we were nearly wiped off the map.

Was our safety a coincidence or calculated? I prefer to think of that brief moment of hesitation as some sort of divine intervention and I lived to know it.

That's why I like this movie. It's about an angel.

＋○＋＋○＋＋○＋

I was in college in the mid-1980s when I first encountered George Bailey. I was living in the dorm, probably watching television to avoid studying for exams. It seems to me there was snow on the ground, and the cool blue-gray sky outside meant it was probably going to snow some more. Perfect weather.

Maybe I was homesick, but all I remember is that it made me choke up, and this film became a Christmas present for me to unwrap every year since then. And I'm not the only one. *It's a Wonderful Life* is America's version of Charles Dickens's *A Christmas Carol*. George Bailey is *our* Ebeneezer Scrooge. Frank Capra's tale, artfully crafted and captured on film, represents a proud and more romantic time in American history.

During the past decade, I've stumbled upon many *Wonderful Life* influences and opportunities, so much so that I thought I'd assemble these sentimental ingredients and present this book to other fans of the film. This is a scrapbook, or, in more contemporary terms, a memory book, filled with nostalgia, trivia, and fascinating images from the film. I want this book to be a historical reference as well as a loving record of reflections contributed by those who helped make this motion picture and those inspired by it.

Call it whatever you want, luck or blessings, but a positive force has acted on this book and led me through my decade-long journey to this point. I was fortunate enough to interview several actors associated with the production, including both George Baileys, young and old. While interviewing Jimmy Stewart about his popular appearances with Johnny Carson for a book I was writing about the *Tonight Show* in 1992, I thought I'd sneak in a few questions regarding his favorite film. I just had to. The wise old actor patiently told me stories I'm sure he'd told countless times before. It was an experience and a privilege I'll never forget.

Few motion pictures have enjoyed such a surprising renaissance as has Frank Capra's masterpiece. Though nominated for five Academy Awards, it was dismissed as a syrupy Christmas tale and doomed for obscurity until bells rang and television gave it wings and a redemption like no other. Today, *It's a Wonderful Life* is an unparalleled, majestic American tradition, almost as much a part of Christmas as the man in the red suit himself. Nearly sixty years later, the film stands in a class by itself, considered a classic by most. This black and white beauty has won the respect of generations of fans and film historians alike.

You may be surprised how completely *It's a Wonderful Life* has permeated our society and our holiday season, and positively impacted the lives of its cast members. These pages contain more than memoirs of the cast and Frank Capra. With this memory book, I hope to dispel a few myths about this film that have surfaced over time, as well as present a fresh approach from some insightful writers who tackle this film's powerful legacy. This book is for all who have fallen under its spell, for all who love its earthy, old-fashioned feel, and for those whose lives have been enriched by its simple philosophies.

And best of all, I'm excited to unveil some rare unpublished photographs taken during the filming of scenes that were eventually cut from the final version. These unseen gems, culled from a variety of archives and private sources, are simply extraordinary. Like Clarence warned, "You'll see a lot of strange things from now on." I trust that these behind-the-scenes glimpses will inspire you to rediscover *It's a Wonderful Life* in a way you haven't before. In some respects, this book is a look back into the mysterious world of what-if. Angels included.

Steve Cox

It's a Wonderful Life

1

'*S* wonderful . . . '*Smarvelous*

It's got everything in it. It's innocent, it's mythological. It's a
rich film; it's a film that both Jimmy Stewart and Frank Capra
have to be proud of. I hope to God I make a movie like that one
day.

                                         —RICHARD DREYFUSS

It's a Wonderful Life has had a most amazing life. Probably more
than any other film that Hollywood has given us, this classic
has endured because of its unique life, death, and rebirth. Even
today, nearly sixty years after it premiered in December 1946,
viewers relive it every year at holiday time. In the landscape of
American motion pictures, *It's a Wonderful Life* shines like a bril-
liant illuminated angel atop Tinseltown's Christmas tree, noble
and towering above the rest.

Most ironic perhaps is that the film was never intended to
be a Christmas flick. Frank Capra, the film's director and producer, and really its driving force, knew he had something special in this story, a powerful message that needed to be
expressed with the right touch. Like his film *Meet John Doe*, he
put this dark tale of George Bailey within the framework of our
most popular holiday for a reason: "Christmas makes people
vulnerable, brings out deep feelings. No one is neutral. People

This rare candid shot captures Frank Capra deep in thought on the Bedford Falls street set. By the time he launched Liberty films with *It's a Wonderful Life*, Capra had won three Oscars for his direction of *It Happened One Night* (1934), *Mr. Deeds Goes to Town* (1936), and *You Can't Take It With You* (1938).

either feel more joyous or sadder. It's a time when some people feel lonelier, more abandoned. There are many suicides that time of year."

Not instantly, but mysteriously, the saga of George Bailey in Bedford Falls became one of America's black and white treasures, and stands as a grand achievement not only for its stars but for the director who was successful in applying that magic touch—that Capra touch. Was the movie an accidental triumph? Or did it have some heavenly help? Was he merely playing with our collective emotions or did he strike a chord that needed striking?

Both Frank Capra and Jimmy Stewart had just returned from their service in World War II; both were physically and emotionally sensitive at the time, maybe even mentally exhausted. Stewart came back a bona fide decorated war hero, but he was ready to forget his past and get on with his film career. They felt no different from the rest of America at that time—eager for a new start. Stewart did not want to give any appearance of trying to trade on his war record. In fact, he was so sensitive to this that when he signed on for *It's a Wonderful Life,* he had a clause inserted in his contract forbidding the exploitation of his war fame.

Capra had already been directing for some twenty years when he organized Liberty Films after the war and affiliated his first production with RKO Pictures. His first film following the War was to be *It's a Wonderful Life,* and Stewart, already an Academy Award winner himself, would star in the film. Capra knew that America desperately needed its spirits lifted at this crucial time. "People are numb after the catastrophic events of the past ten to fifteen years," he told the *L.A. Times* in early 1946. "I would not attempt to reach them mentally through a picture, only emotionally."

There's no revisionism here. Capra had a specific goal with this motion picture and he did not hesitate mapping it out. As he told writer Edwin Schallert in

Stewart and Capra work out a scene on the set of Mary Hatch's foyer.

Wonderful Possibilities

. . . That's an idea . . . all right. You've got your wish. You've never been born.

↜Clarence

Let's pretend *It's a Wonderful Life* hadn't been "born" and casting was still under way. Who would you place in these roles? It's hard to imagine anyone playing these parts other than the ensemble Frank Capra brought together. But Capra did have his lists, you know. The choices weren't as effortless as you may think.

For the role of George Bailey, Capra has stated that he always had Jimmy Stewart in mind, although, he concedes, Henry Fonda was in the running. Stewart had more of a natural quality that the director preferred and the two had already worked well together in two films, *You Can't Take It With You* (1938) and *Mr. Smith Goes to Washington* (1939). Writer Michael Sragow acknowledges that by the time Stewart became George Bailey, his style "hadn't yet stiffened into the head-scratching, hemming and hawing mannerisms when he made this movie (after his return from years in military service); neither his persona nor his acting had turned to mush. On screen he still had as much lightness as warmth, as much gentle restraint as enthusiasm."

Next, Capra offered the role of Mary Hatch to actress Jean Arthur, his first choice. Arthur had romanced Stewart in *Mr. Smith*; however, the actress turned the role down due to a prior commitment of starring in a Garson Kanin play on Broadway. Casting the role of Mary was a bit of a headache for Capra. Olivia DeHavilland was considered, as were Martha Scott and Ann

Dvorak. Ultimately, Capra went to MGM and "borrowed" Donna Reed, a fresh-faced actress whom he knew would add sweetness and innocence to the role of young Mary Hatch.

For the detestable Mr. Potter (originally dubbed Herbert Potter, not Henry Potter), Capra considered a few debonair types such as Louis Calhern, Raymond Massey, and Claude Rains. Also on the list to play Potter were Edgar Buchanan, Vincent Price, Victor Jory, Edward Arnold, Charles Bickford, and

Thirty-year-old Jimmy Stewart poses patiently for MGM's famed photographer, Clarence Sinclair Bull, in 1939.

"Welcome home, Mr. Bailey."

Thomas Mitchell (who eventually won the role of Uncle Billy). Finally, Capra borrowed Lionel Barrymore from MGM to handle the evil Potter.

Old Man Gower was also a toughie to cast. Capra had some great character actors in mind: Donald Meek, Charles Grapewin, Samuel Hinds, Percy Kilbride, Guy Kibbee, Jean Hershholt, John Qualen, Harry Davenport, and even Henry Travers (who eventually received the role of Clarence). It was a gamble for Capra to place seasoned actor H. B. Warner in the role of Mr. Gower, the druggist. Known at the time for his dignified performances (as well as his celebrated portrayal of Christ in Cecil B. DeMille's 1927 silent film *King of Kings*), Warner was openly delighted to work with Capra. He told reporters at the time, "Twenty years ago DeMille typed me and I've been typed ever since. Lost hundreds of jobs. C. B. will die when he sees me playing a bum in Capra's new picture . . . I'm playing the damndest dirtiest bum you ever saw, a proper drunk, thanks to Capra, who used a little imagination."

W. C. Fields made Capra's list of possibilities to play the original silly old fool, Uncle Billy. So did Donald Meek, Hugh Herbert, Frank Morgan, Walter Brennan, Ernest Treux, Henry Travers, Charles Ruggles, and Adolphe Menjou.

Budding starlet Gloria Grahame, a green-eyed blonde, was just twenty years old when she landed the part of small-town floozie Violet Bick, her first major film role. According to press articles at the time, Grahame felt she was being ignored at MGM when Capra borrowed her for *Wonderful Life*. When MGM head Louis B. Mayer discovered that outside studios were capitalizing on "their discovery," they immediately snatched her back and assigned her to two films, *Merton of the Movies* and *It Happened in Brooklyn*. Grahame was perfect as the "good bad girl," just the type that Capra was searching for to add sexual allure to the role. (Years later, Grahame explained her raw appeal: "It wasn't the way I looked at a man, but the thought behind it.")

By the end of April 1946, the film had been cast—a task that Capra fulfilled mostly on his own. Although he worked with casting agents to procure talent, the choices were purely his own, even down to the smallest roles. Yes, Capra even hired the midgets who would work as the children's stand-ins on the film. Charlotte Sullivan, Nels Nelson, Henry Stone, and Luz Potter, all midget actors who also worked as stunt-doubles, were hired to work on the set when the children were at school. "Frank

Old codger Charles Coburn as Mr. Potter?

Menacing Vincent Price as Mr. Potter?

Scene-stealing Hattie McDaniel as Annie the cook?

Taciturn Raymond Massey as Mr. Potter?

Blustery Frank Morgan as Uncle Billy?

Willful Clara Blandick as Annie the cook?

Capra was great to work with," said Nels Nelson in 1989. "Most of my work involved standing in for the little kids in the house scene where Jimmy Stewart comes in raging mad. We'd be there so the technicians could light the set and approximate the movements of the kids. Capra was so easy-going, not like most of the directors I've worked with over the years. I loved that job." (Just a few years prior, both Sullivan and Nelson had worked together as Munchkins in the MGM film classic *The Wizard of Oz*, and they continued in motion picture work for the rest of their lives.)

Perky Irene Ryan as Annie the cook?

Brawny Barton MacLane as Bert the cop?

Flirty Iris Adrian as Violet Bick?

Malevolent Claude Rains as Mr. Potter?

Delicate Olivia de Havilland as Mary Hatch?

Creepy John Carradine as the voice of Joseph in Heaven?

Folksy yokel Percy Kilbride as Mr. Gower?

Pokey Charley Grapewin as Mr. Gower?

Absurdly agitated W. C. Fields as Uncle Billy?

Look closely: As an amusing in-joke and for the sake of fastidiousness, Frank Capra decorated Mr. Bailey's desk with an actual portrait of Jimmy Stewart as a toddler on a tricycle. "That's remarkable," stated Stewart when he stared at these two photographs in 1991. "I don't know that I was ever aware of this fact, even back then. Frank was full of surprises, that's why we got along so famously."

March 1946, weeks before cameras even began rolling, there were two things he wished to accomplish with *It's a Wonderful Life*: "One is to strengthen the individual's belief in himself and the other, even more important right now, is to combat a modern trend toward atheism which is very much present in the world." And he wished to do it with an angel named Clarence.

Yes, the director wanted to entertain, but in so doing he also wished to make a positive statement with his work. "Improving the individual and bringing a more hopeful outlook on life," he said, was all part of it.

The Italian-born film director who gave us gems like *Mr. Smith Goes to Washington* and *You Can't Take It With You* retired much too soon in his career. *It's a Wonderful Life* was one of his final films. Capra was known as "Hollywood's poet of the common man" in the 1930s, when he served up those charming movies full of decency and human spirit that inspired millions. During the Depression his Clark Gable and Claudette Colbert romp, *It Happened One Night*, gave the public a terrific boost in morale.

*W*hat is remarkable about *It's a Wonderful Life* is how well it holds up over the years; it's one of those timeless movies, like *Casablanca* or *The Third Man*, that improve with age. Some movies, even good ones, should be seen only once. When we know how they turn out, they've surrendered their mystery and appeal. Other movies can be viewed an indefinite number of times. *It's a Wonderful Life* falls in the second category.

—Roger Ebert, *TV Guide*, December 1988

He happily lived to see *Wonderful Life*—his favorite of his films—win an overwhelming rediscovery in the 1980s and earn the respect he knew it deserved. Capra smiled as he watched his movie take on a monumental status blessed with the label "classic"; and he cringed when it fell victim to meddlers who painted it with "Easter egg colors" during the dastardly experimental film-colorization phase of the late 1980s.

The story and legacy of this film is atypical, a masterpiece essentially lost and then rediscovered decades later. And yet, so little behind-the-scenes texture has been unearthed and published about this warhorse, which, even today, carries enough might to air on prime-time television annually. Hopefully, this memory book

Academy Award–winning screen composer Dimitri Tiomkin, one of Hollywood's most honored—with an astounding twenty-three Oscar nominations in his illustrious career—created a unique score for *It's a Wonderful Life*. It was a dark masterpiece that Tiomkin blended with the action to parallel the somber near-suicidal story, but much of it never made it in the final film. Recorded in November of 1946, the film's score reflected and complemented the period moments of Americana illustrating the passage of time that sweeps through the life of George Bailey.

Tiomkin's collaborative work alongside Frank Capra proved highly successful in several motion pictures (including *Lost Horizon* and *Mr. Smith Goes to Washington*) prior to World War II. Capra respected Tiomkin's flavoring in all of the films he scored, but their friendship nearly ended following *It's a Wonderful Life*. The film that eventually became one of Tiomkin's most famous works actually became a disappointment for the composer, both personally and professionally, when Capra replaced much of his original orchestration with existing cue music from other sources. For instance, Tiomkin's original ending of the film featured "Ode to Joy" from Beethoven's Ninth Symphony, but was replaced with "Auld Lang Syne."

In his autobiography, *Please Don't Hate Me,* published in 1959, the composer claimed never to have sat and watched the entire film after completion. "After the music was on the soundtrack, Frank [Capra] cut it, switched sections around, and patched it up, an all-round scissors job. After that I didn't want to hear it," Tiomkin admitted. "Frank and I had no wrangle about the matter. I said nothing. We simply didn't see each other for a year and a half."

For the saga of George Bailey, the Russian-born composer created a rich and complex score that followed the scope of emotions, the highs and lows of the film's moods and attitudes. But because the film was pushed up and the film's distributor, RKO, decided to rush release of the movie just before Christmas in 1946, Capra wanted to brighten moments of the film's mood and excised many of Tiomkin's cues.

In the late 1980s, film and music producer Willard Carroll discovered Tiomkin's entire original score for *It's a Wonderful Life* while exploring the archives at the University of Southern California. Carroll, along with composer and conductor David

Discontented, Oscar-winning film composer Dimitri Tiomkin never wanted to watch It's a Wonderful Life *again after scoring the film.*

Newman, set out to release the unaltered Tiomkin score. In 1988, their CD (which also includes suites from *Miracle on 34th Street* and *A Christmas Carol*) was released by Telarc, with music richly recreated and recorded by London's Royal Philharmonic Orchestra.

"The score as it stands in the movie is a hodgepodge," explains Carroll. "Most of it is Tiomkin, but because of the accelerated release date, a great deal of it was chopped up, switched around, and in many cases, replaced by cues from other movies. The major piece of music near the end of the film ("Hallelujah"), for example, was Alfred Newman's score for *The Hunchback of Notre Dame,* used in place of Tiomkin's cues.

"We recorded the complete score as Tiomkin originally intended it, unheard since 1946."

Tiomkin's disappointment with Capra's film was a mere page out of his life and memoirs. Tiomkin, whose nickname to friends was "Timmy," died in London on November 11, 1979. The versatile composer and pianist's career was filled with decorated achievements including golden Oscar statuettes for his scores for *High Noon*—along with a Best Song Oscar for "Do Not Forsake Me, Oh My Darlin'" (1952)—*The High and the Mighty* (1954), and *The Old Man and the Sea* (1958). He also contributed scores and musical selections to a formidable list of films including *Great Catherine* (1968), *The War Wagon* (1967), *The Fall of the Roman Empire* (1964), *The Guns of Navarone* (1961), *The Alamo* (1960), *Rio Bravo* (1959), *Search for Paradise* (1957), *Giant* (1956), *Land of the Pharaohs* (1955), *Strange Lady in Town* (1955), *Dial M for Murder* (1954), *Jeopardy* (1953), *Return to Paradise* (1953), *Angel Face* (1952), *The Happy Time* (1952), *The Big Sky* (1952), *Drums in the Deep South* (1951), *Strangers on a Train* (1951), *Cyrano de Bergerac* (1950), *Guilty Bystander* (1950), *So This Is New York* (1948), *Portrait of Jennie* (1948), *Tarzan and the Mermaids* (1948), *Duel in the Sun* (1946), *The Dark Mirror* (1946), *Angel on My Shoulder* (1946), *Black Beauty* (1946), *The Imposter* (1944), *Twin Beds* (1942), *Meet John Doe* (1941), *Lucky Partners* (1940), *Only Angels Have Wings* (1939), *You Can't Take It With You* (1938), *I Live My Life* (1935), *Roast Beef and Movies* (1934), *Alice in Wonderland* (1933), and *Crazy House* (1930).

will shed some light on just why movie fans everywhere have embraced its message so and fallen under its spell.

❈❈❈❈

Wonderful things surfaced during the research for this memory book: some rare, unpublished photographs which documented filmed scenes that were left on the cutting room floor, plus some images never before published of the talents who created this matchless movie. There are surprises. Did you realize that opera-trained Adriana Caselotti (the memorable voice of Walt Disney's Snow White) sings in this film? At the beginning of the story, as we get acquainted with the life of George Bailey, just who were the heavenly voices who narrate the opening? For years, people assumed the voices were supposed to be God and another angel named Joseph. Well, that wasn't really the way it was written. The faceless actors who spoke from the heavens were never included in the film's credits . . . until now. (*Hint:* One of the actors was the voice of the Magic Mirror in *Snow White and the Seven Dwarfs.*) Which scene was Jimmy Stewart's favorite? And whatever happened to those Bailey kids? Where are they today? What East Coast city was Frank Capra's inspiration for small town Bedford Falls? And why did Frank Capra cut a vital scene where Mr. Potter gets scolded?

An autographed portrait of one of MGM's most bankable stars in the 1930s and '40s, the great Lionel Barrymore.

Served with a Twist

For those few who have angrily slumped into bed each Christmas like Scrooge—not even turning on the television—here's the story of *It's a Wonderful Life*. And for those who are just discovering it, Kenneth Turan eloquently summarized the plot and revealed why this movie is so special in a 1989 *TV Guide* holiday feature article.

> Most critics view *It's a Wonderful Life* as of a piece with the other Capra vehicles such as *Mr. Smith Goes to Washington* and *Mr. Deeds Goes to Town*—stories of civic idealism versus the entrenched forces of corruption—but in fact it works precisely the same way *A Christmas Carol* does, with one very crucial twist.
>
> In despair on Christmas Eve, the happiest night of the year, normally decent citizen George Bailey turns into a mini-Scrooge. He bitterly calls his uncle a "silly, stupid old fool," devastates his family with brutal irony, brusquely complains to his wife, "Why do we have to have all these kids?" and violently knocks over a table, spilling its contents to the floor. Having Jimmy Stewart, usually the picture of heedless optimism, perpetrate this kind of sacrilege makes the scene all the more effective.
>
> Brought to the brink of suicide by the possibility of undeserved financial ruin, Bailey, like Scrooge, is allowed to step outside the boundaries of space and time and see the truth about his life. But while Scrooge sees what a monster he's been, George Bailey sees that all the sacrifices he's made, all the good deeds he thought were unrequited, have brought him the kind of love and respect mere money can never hope to buy. His best, most unselfish actions are all rewarded, just like we hope ours will be. By offering everyone this kind of redemption and reward, *It's a Wonderful Life* has become the Christmas film for all seasons.

⊹⊹⊹⊹

The story of *It's a Wonderful Life* began as a Christmas card. Well, actually more like a pamphlet than a card. The concept was conceived by thirty-eight-year-old Philip Van Doren Stern, a noted American history buff, who thought of it in his bathroom one morning.

Stern, a successful author of several books by 1946, related the impetus for his tale of hopelessness in an article published in the *New York Herald Tribune*, just as the film adaptation of his story was being released: "It began nearly eight years ago," Stern explained, "on February 12, 1938, to be exact. That morning while I was shaving, I got an idea for a story. The idea came to me complete from start to finish—a most unusual occurrence, as any writer will tell you, for ordinarily a story has to be struggled with, changed around and fixed up."

Fresh from shaving, Stern sat down and typed out a two-page outline, dated it, and then put the pages in a file. The story about an ordinary man who wishes he'd never been born and is given the chance to see how different the world would be without his presence was a haunting premise for Stern. During the next several years he attempted to flesh out the details, but he was unsatisfied each

At a party thrown by Liberty Films to launch its first production, *It's a Wonderful Life*, are Lionel Barrymore, Frank Capra, Donald Crisp, and H. B. Warner (December 1946).

"Buffalo Gals"

Although much of his original score had been cut, the film's composer, Dimitri Tiomkin, incorporated some recognizable cues in the film, including "Twinkle Twinkle" (for Clarence's ethereal moments), "My Wild Irish Rose" (Uncle Billy's inebriated stupor), "The Wedding March," "The Charleston," and other known suites and themes. One of the most popular themes to come out of the film is "Buffalo Gals," which George and Mary share as a romantic tune together.

"Buffalo Gals (Won't You Come Out Tonight?)" is an oldie dating back to the mid-1800s, popular in minstrel shows before the Civil War, with lyrics written by Cool White. It was also a popular cowboy song that originally went by the title "Lubly Fan." (Oddly, the tune "Lubly Fan" is mentioned in Mark Twain's *Tom Sawyer,* which, of course, is the book Clarence totes around in *It's a Wonderful Life.*) The

song became so popular in certain regions of the country, it was frequently refashioned in each of the localities, such as "Pittsburgh Gals," or "Louisiana Gals."

In the mid-1940s the song was adapted and retitled again as "Dance With a Dolly

(With a Hole in Her Stocking)." In 1944 Russ Morgan and his Orchestra recorded a best-selling version of this song (for Decca) which made the Hit Parade; the song can also be heard in the films *Strictly in the Groove* (1942), *On Stage Everybody* (1945), *Her Lucky Night* (1945, sung by the Andrews Sisters), and *Cow Town* (1950).

"Buffalo Gals can't you come out tonight . . . and dance by the light of the moon." Things spark for Mary and George in this oddly romantic scene amidst the hydrangea bushes.

Jimmy Stewart and Frank Capra, both fresh from military duty and equally nervous, wanted to put the war behind them and help Americans do the same. And they had a feeling they'd be creating something magical with this angelic script.

Clarence spooks the
toll-bridge operator
(Tom Fadden).

time and repeatedly put the story back on the shelf. Finally, in the
spring of 1943, he dusted off the manuscript once again, this time
adding a Christmas background and giving it a title: "The Greatest
Gift." He hoped that a magazine editor might buy it as fantasy fic-
tion, but he was unable to sell the story. So he revised it again and
spent his own money printing it as a twenty-four-page pamphlet,
which he presented to friends and mailed out to relatives around the
country as Christmas greetings that year—something a little meatier
than just a card with a two-line salutation.

"I remember when I received mine," said Miriam Stern, the
youngest sister of Philip. "I was road manager for Sammy Kaye's
orchestra and we were in California in 1943, and it was the first time
in my life I was homesick. When I received Phil's story, I cried. It was
a totally original idea."

The Bailey family
takes pictures on
the front porch.

*Noooope, nope,
nope.* George
doesn't want the
suitcase fitted up
with combs and
brushes.

The pamphlet also landed in the hands of a Hollywood agent who was struck by its originality and managed to get the story sold to Cary Grant's agent. Philip Van Doren Stern soon received a check for $10,000, and during the next few years the story was shifted around from one owner to another. Several writers toiled with the story and rewrote versions based on Stern's concept, but none were filmed. Reportedly, Howard Hughes had interest in it briefly. But finally, in 1946, Frank Capra read the story and immediately became intrigued. He, along with his newly formed Liberty Films, purchased the rights from RKO Radio Pictures. Together with writers Frances Goodrich and Albert Hackett (a married writing team who'd written other scripts, including *The Thin Man*), Capra finally adapted it into *It's a Wonderful Life*.

Capra brought in several more writers who contributed to polishing the script (including Jo Swerling, Michael Wilson, and Dorothy Parker) and this conglomeration of talents caused some contention. The Screen Writers Guild was forced to step in with arbitration and Jo Swerling received credit for "additional scenes." The Hacketts were never happy with Capra's changes to their script as well as the addition of Swerling to the project. The couple felt the entire situation was uncomfortable and became angry with Capra; for many years, the embittered writing team refused to see *It's a Wonderful Life*. According to sources in their family, the Hacketts never forgave Capra for having other writers rework their script, and following the experience they never worked with him again. They went on to pen screenplays for fourteen more films, including *Easter Parade, Father of*

> *C*apra returned to the writing of the story with Goodrich and Hackett. He called in Jo Swerling to write additional scenes and there emerged the tender dramatic story of a young American and his dreams; his attempts to escape from the small town and go to the big city; his marriage to his child-hood sweetheart, his family and the final realization that his life, despite his failings and doubts, had been a full and successful one as measured by the yardstick of humanity. . . .
>
> ↭ *It's a Wonderful Life* PRESS CAMPAIGN BOOKLET

Mary and George share in a phone conversation that ends in a heated embrace.

the Bride and its sequel, *Father's Little Dividend*, and *Seven Brides for Seven Brothers*. According to their nephew, David Goodrich, their proudest writing achievement was their 1955 play, *The Diary of Anne Frank*, which was awarded the Pulitzer Prize for drama.

Following casting, Capra was ready to construct his fictional town of Bedford Falls, New York. Jack Okey and Emile Kuri were assigned to create this mythical town on a four-acre site at the RKO Ranch in Encino, California. They built this quaint faux town, which included a main street three hundred yards long, with a tree-shaded center parkway running its entire length. It included a factory district, slums, and a residential section. According to a press release for the film, "Months before a camera was turned on, pigeons, dogs, and cats were housed on the mammoth set so that when production actually got under way, they would feel at home and lend a realistic touch to the town."

The set itself was an ever-changing complexity. The town of Bedford Falls goes through a lapse of years and seasons, and these details required huge amounts of manpower and effort to keep up. On main street, the store windows had to be redressed, older signs had to be changed to neon-lit spectacles for George's nightmarish tour through Pottersville. Rain, snow, and weather alterations took time and a team of highly experienced technicians.

Frank Capra never confirmed it, but for many years the rumor has been that his inspiration for the town of Bedford Falls was a little town in upstate New York called Seneca Falls. Capra reportedly had an aunt who lived in a nearby town and he visited the quaint area many times. (Neighboring cities like Elmira, Syracuse, and Rochester are mentioned in the film.) Seneca Falls remains to this day a charmer. The streets are lined with old Victorian houses that resemble the movie's Granville house at 320 Sycamore; its Main Street is illuminated at night with rows of old-fashioned black lampposts. The town still has its old railroad station, and during the coldest winter months, the lake freezes over, perfect for hockey and sledding. Most eerie, however, is the old Seneca Falls bridge, a steel girder structure exactly like the one that George Bailey stopped at for his life-altering experience in *It's a Wonderful Life*.

Karolyn Grimes, who played Zuzu in the film, was invited to visit Seneca Falls during a wintry Christmas season in 2002. "I could see what had been described to me," she says, "that Seneca Falls is an industrial town much like Bedford Falls, with factories that once gave employment to the Italian immigrant population. Even though I never had visited before, the people in Seneca Falls and in surrounding towns made me feel like this was a homecoming. I felt it the first day . . . in a sense, I was 'home'."

That Capra Technique

They called it "Capra Corn." *It's a Wonderful Life* was a Frank Capra production in every sense and the final product revealed that magic touch. Corny maybe. Heart wrenching—sometimes. Successful . . . always.

Although the Oscar-winning director was admittedly nervous about returning to the camera after five years, shaky about whether he still had the talent for it, he took control and saw this $2 million film through the rain and the snow with confidence. Much later Capra admitted that the film epitomized everything he'd been trying to do and trying to say in other films, only this production accomplished it "very dramatically with a unique story." This was his baby, and, as it turned out, one of his final film creations. Some call it a masterpiece.

Young Associated Press reporter Bob Thomas visited the set of *Wonderful Life* and reported his observations of Capra in a *Hollywood Citizen News* story in July 1946, adding that Capra preferred to work off the home lot of RKO because "there are too many people," the director told him. He rarely hosted visitors, and only an occasional reporter. "The director prefers to shoot away from the studio and even then he often excludes everybody from the set except himself and the actors. Using the script only as a guide, he will work on a scene until it is right, then call back the crew and film it.

"When I saw him at work," Thomas ended his story, "he was conferring with James Stewart and Donna Reed on how she should break the news that she was going to have a baby. They bounced on a bed and bandied suggestions for almost an hour. For all I know, they might still be there."

Capra was an approachable type who remained open to suggestions at work. Remembers Donna Reed in an article the actress wrote about the making of the film in 1975: "On the set, Capra was untiring, with a commanding personality, and his hand-picked crews and cast liked him enormously. He was quick to laugh, given to salty quips, but quick to return to the seriousness of film work. He was quick and generous in his appreciation of a scene that satisfied him. His face hid nothing, revealed everything. He had the rare courage to 'make things up' as we went along, depart from the script, even close down the set for a day to think out scenes.

Anyone with an idea was welcomed, in fact encouraged, to present it. Capra had great courage in his creative convictions, but if he was uncertain about a scene or idea, he also had the courage to admit that he needed time to think (rare!), and then took it (rarer!).

—Donna Reed, March 1975

The element of surprise was not beyond Capra. Writer Nord Riley watched Capra direct the scene where a group of worried depositors crowd the lobby of the Building & Loan hoping to withdraw their money. "To lend added realism," Riley noted, "Capra, without warning, set off a fire siren in the midst of Stewart's speech. The startled cast abandoned Jimmy to rush to the windows to see the blaze, leaving him waving his long arms at their backs. Stewart gulped, matched the siren, roar for roar, and actually won his audience back while the camera ground on.

"Capra has been driving the not-unwilling Stewart without mercy, wringing the utmost out of him by methods that range from trickery to endless rehearsals. At times, he has tossed Jimmy into scenes cold, saying, 'Make up your own dialogue as you go along.

Just say whatever seems natural, the first thing that comes into your head.'"

It was with a gentle hand that Capra pulled the action out of the children working in the film, a delicate process as any director will admit. "There was a lot of love between Frank and his actors," says Bob Anderson, who portrayed young George when he was just twelve years old. "The girls and I, he always hugged us. When we did the drug-store scene he'd have us sit on the stools and we'd rehearse the scene together."

❦❦❦❦

On April 15, 1946, Capra gave the go-ahead for the cameras to roll. The "champagne shot," or the first shot of the movie to be filmed, took place at the Beverly Hills High School "swim gym," where, still today, an actual swimming pool lies under the convertible basketball court. It was a tricky shoot that took three days in the gym because of the number of people in the shot and the complex lighting it required. (A soundstage would have proper tracks for lighting any area, but this required special concessions.) For the most part, the entire film was shot on Soundstage 14 at the RKO-Pathé Studios

Ms. Jean McDaniel, an eighty-seven-year-old retired teacher, visits her former pupil, director Frank Capra, on the set. When he heard that his former fifth-grade teacher had never visited a motion picture studio, Capra invited her to tour the lot and be his guest for lunch.

(now known as the Culver Studios) in Culver City, California. Exteriors of Bedford Falls took place on the specially constructed set on the RKO Ranch, with the exception of a few on-location shots in Southern California such as the Martini housewarming ceremony (in La Crescenta, California) and the train station scene (at the Pasadena train station).

Filming lasted exactly ninety days, right on schedule, and concluded on Saturday, July 27, 1946. The film exceeded its budget at a cost of more than $3 million. Although Capra attempted to shoot the movie in sequence where possible, scenes inevitably had to be filmed on certain sets during certain blocks of days to take advantage of calculated elements such as the weather.

The final action of the film, commonly known as the "martini shot" (for the cocktail, not the character of Mr. Martini) was a "process shot" that took place on the soundstage. It's the scene where Mary and George are inside Ernie's cab, fresh from their wedding and eager to get started on their honeymoon. They are peering out the back window of the cab while rain pours over Bedford Falls. Ernie says, "I've never really seen one, but that's got all the earmarks of a run."

George hesitatingly decides to get out of the cab and investigate.

"Please, let's not stop, George." Mary pleads.

"I'll be back in a minute, Mary." George says.

Capra, satisfied with the last shot, called out "Cut . . . that's a wrap!" and *It's a Wonderful Life* was in the can. The rain was called to a halt, lights went up in the soundstage and there was a boom of applause all around. Before getting out of the cab, Donna Reed and Jimmy Stewart smiled and hugged each other and promised to stay in touch.

A Stern Storyteller

In 1984, all of the obituaries prominently noted the same thing: Philip Van Doren Stern, eighty-three, novelist and historian whose brief Christmas story was the inspiration for the film *It's a Wonderful Life,* died July 31 in Sarasota, Florida.

He probably would have cringed at his own newspaper obits that attempted to recount his life and career. Granted, *It's a Wonderful Life* has become an entrenched part of American culture, yet so few people—even today—are conscious of who wrote the tale. But there was so much more to the author. Philip Van Doren Stern was one of the most influential Civil War historians of the twentieth century and his little Christmas story, "The Greatest Gift," is just a small part of his successful career as a typographer, journalist, historian, and author. Stern was also a complex man, a great explorer of the mind with a penchant for examining the darker side of life.

He was born in Wyalusing, Pennsylvania, but grew up in New Jersey, attended

A rare portrait of the man who wrote "The Greatest Gift," prolific author Philip Van Doren Stern.

Rutgers University, and graduated in 1924 with a degree in Liberal Arts. Next to a small, pensive portrait of the young man in spectacles, his graduating yearbook entry reads:

> "No, I don't think much of the present day American writers," objects Stern, our aspiring literary critique. Whereupon we quite gave up any hope of pleasing him with this bit of dissertation. His tastes are ultra-artistic and far too high to be realized by our own efforts. . . . His chief ambition is to translate the various phases of life he sees, into some form of literature, new and original. We can well imagine him living the colorful life of Greenwich Village. . . .

One of his earliest jobs in publishing was as a typographer for Simon and Schuster publishers in New York. He eventually laid down blueprints for the craft in the book *An Introduction to Typography,* which became quite valuable in the trade. Stern also worked as an editor for Pocket Books and Alfred A. Knopf publishers, but it was his work as a historian that most satisfied his urges and took advantage of his talents. A journalist at heart, he began preparing books about American history and spent many years traveling the United States researching his interests, evolving into an authority on the Civil War and that era, and later penning several respected nonfiction books, including *The Man Who Killed Lincoln* (1939), *The Life & Writings of Abraham Lincoln* (1940), *Civil War Christmas Album* (1951), *Robert E. Lee: The Man & The Soldier* (1963), *An End to Valor: The Last Days of the Civil War* (1958), and *The Confederate Navy* (1962).

Literary critic Jessica Salmonson noted: "His novel *The Drums of Morning* is regarded as one of the great novels about the abolitionist movement and vastly preferred over *Gone With the Wind* by anyone with even a little real knowledge of the Civil War."

And then there was the other side of Stern, the dark side. The part of this mysterious man that appreciated the bizarre and the macabre, partial to mind-bending stories of gore and horror. This was the deep curiosity that welled up inside him and eerily prompted his tale of suicide and rebirth one morning . . . a concept that eventually inspired *It's a Wonderful Life.*

It's no surprise that he was a devoted fan of Edgar Allan Poe, having published essays on the mystery writer and edited the book *The Portable Poe* (1945). Stern loved the twisted, the ghostly, and the fantastic. Long before Americans got caught up in Rod Serling's *Twilight Zone,* readers enjoyed Stern's major anthologies, such as *The Midnight Reader* (1942, also issued as The Pocket Book of Ghost Stories: Great Stories of Haunting and Horror), *The Moonlight Traveler: Great Tales of Fantasy and Imagination* (1943), *Travelers in Time: Strange Tales of Man's Journeys into the Past & the Future* (1947), *The Other Side of the Clock: Stories Out of Time, Out of Place* (1969), *Strange Beasts & Unnatural Monsters* (1968).

Stern knew that without a free flow of the imagination, stories like the sad tale of George Bailey and Bedford Falls would have never emerged. He possessed an intellectual sentiment for the human imagination as well as for our fascination with darkness and the unknown. The writer eloquently probed these areas in an article titled "The Enjoyment of Horror," published in the *Rutgers Alumni Monthly,* January 1946. Enter his dimension for a moment. Although he bowed to the "age-old mysteries of the origin of life and meaning of death," he also declared that there are "demons and ghosts . . . they are bred of our own imaginings, manufactured from the stuff of dreams.

"In dreams we summon up dark images which the waking mind would not tolerate; in them nothing is too absurd or too horrible to seem true. Imagination, unchecked by reason, runs riot, madly spinning false shapes of desire and fear. The sane banish their dream creations each morning—the insane permit them to haunt their daylight hours.

"The subconscious is the lair of creatures which would shame us all if they were ever to see the light of day. Luckily we are able to keep the lid closed down firmly on them; only at night do they escape from their prison to dance their grotesque sarabands while we groan and toss in our sleep. But man, who probes every emotion, from love to murderous hatred, for his literary material, has not neglected even the contents of his most dreadful dreams. In all lands and ages he has drawn upon them for legends of haunting and horror."

One of Capra's Darker Scenes

Veteran actor H. B. Warner was the perfect choice for Mr. Gower, a delicate role that required a versatile performer who could effortlessly siphon just enough sympathy from his audience while doing seemingly unlikable things, and later be as lovable as a proud grandfather. In one scene he's the drunken, disheveled pharmacist who is torn up by the sudden news of the death of his son. Later he's sober and sentimental. Warner beautifully handled the spectrum of emotions of the man: the menacing, the pathetic, the grateful.

An old man himself at that time, H. B. was a distinguished actor from the silent film era who was thrilled to work with Capra. The role called for Warner to plumb the depths of his talents in the tense opening scene where he drunkenly spars with his young co-actor.

Bobbie Anderson remembers that Warner, a true "method" actor, went off to himself and began nipping the hard stuff early on the day they shot the memorable scene. Capra knew what he was doing when he let Warner alone with his little bottle until the old actor was ripe. "He started drinking in the morning and was nipping all day," says Anderson. "We didn't get to filming the sequences until like three o'clock in the afternoon."

It doesn't matter how many times you've watched *It's a Wonderful Life*. That intense moment when an agitated Mr. Gower delivers those whacks to George's trick ear makes you wince as much as the little girl watching from the drugstore does.

"He actually bloodied my ear," Anderson recalls with the same pleasant raspy edge in his voice that he had as a youngster.

"That was Capra's idea of getting it to the Academy Award point. We didn't do anything else that day. We rehearsed, and as the day progressed, the louder and more demanding H. B. got. We'd rest for a little while; I'd go back to school. They'd bring me back out and we'd spar a little more. It wasn't that I wanted to keep going back into that room. I figured after the third round, I'd had enough."

Well after lunchtime, the cameras rolled. This time, Anderson recalls, Stewart stood next to Capra, both eyeing the big moment with great expectation. It took just minutes to capture one of the film's most disturbing scenes.

A portrait of a pensive H. B. Warner, traditionally a serious actor who won acclaim when he portrayed Jesus Christ in the 1927 silent epic King of Kings.

"My ear was beat up and my face was red and I was in tears. I knew when I went through the door of that drugstore to go behind those pillboxes, I was gonna get knocked on my butt, and it was an emotional high.

"I was a baby," he says. "I didn't know what we were building for. H. B. was perfect. He reached the crescendo. At the end, when it was all over, he was very lovable. He grabbed me and hugged me and he meant it."

As the day went on, Capra allowed actor H. B. Warner to get sufficiently stewed before shooting this climactic scene where Mr. Gower, distraught over his son's death, physically punishes George.

Breaking the Ice

The Italian born director is a stickler for exactitude. In his pictures he always has rain, snow or some other meteorological disturbance that will present a problem for accuracy. In his present "It's a Wonderful Life," he ordered a snowstorm. I saw several blocks of an imitation New York town covered with enough gypsum to build a dozen houses.

᪣BoB Thomas, Associated Press, July 10, 1946

Frank Capra loved using weather in his films as a vital element in the photography as well as in the storyline. He couldn't help but admire the shot of George and Mary peering out the back of the cab as the rain streaked the window like tears during the downpour. The snow-chilled wind at the bridge when George contemplates suicide was shot with just the right amount of moonlit force, Capra thought. Although extremely difficult to film because of the shadows, the snow in the black and white photography only accentuated the contrast and added to the beauty of the scenes. Ansel Adams would've been mighty proud of this backdrop.

With *Wonderful Life,* Capra realistically whisks us through wintry days and hot summer nights, with everything in between. Realism was his challenge. (So detail-oriented was Capra, he made a note in his production diary about the "differences between sound of rain in summer and winter. Rain on leaves makes a different sound than rain on bare limbs.") During the four and a half months of filming—amid sweltering summer months in Southern California, mind you—Bedford Falls goes through about eight "changes of costume" to illustrate the seasons and take the viewer from 1919 to 1946 (the present day when the film debuted) in two hours' time. Without a doubt, this movie can boast some of the most authentic bright snow and gloomy rain to ever season a film.

The RKO press campaign book revealed in 1946 that a technical innovation was introduced in the making of this seasonal flick: "For the first time, a new chemical snow was used instead of the customary corn-flakes for falling snow. Made from a carbon dioxide base, the new snow can be controlled to fall in large, billowy flakes, or, with the aid of wind machines, depict a howling blizzard. Approximately 16,140 gallons of the chemical fluff, 15 carloads of dolomite, twelve thousand 175-pound sacks of asbestos and nearly ten thousand tons of ice were used for the winter scenes."

Yes, it's true that corn flakes (painted white) were commonly used in films back then to simulate snow, and they provided a crunch like snow when walked on—but a little too hearty a crunch for Capra's taste. The director preferred something more realistic and asked the studio's special effects specialists to improve the snow with something more workable.

Bob Lawless, one of the film's special effects technicians, remembers *It's a Wonderful Life* vividly because of the "new" snow developed specifically for this shoot.

"There were three men, Russell Shearman, Marty Martin, and Jack Lannon, who were the head of the department at RKO special effects," he said. "They developed this particular snow that had never been done before.

"The RKO department heads came up with this idea of using foamite, which fire fighters used to put out fires. They mixed it with soap and water and a little plaster, and they shoved it through a high-pressure hose. Very high pressure. Then they used a

George plunges into the drink to save a drowning man.

huge wind machine and they could control the drift of the snow, giving it a violent whirling or a soft touch. And that was the way it was developed, and it is used today throughout the industry. These three men are responsible for this particular snow system."

Lawless, who was in his early twenties at the time, says he worked several days and nights spraying snow all over the streets with Russell Cully and other technicians at the ranch in Encino, California, where Bedford Falls was filmed outdoors. "There was about four acres of ground that they had to cover with gypsum and plaster. The gypsum was used on the window sills and the plaster was built up on the banks and then they used about three hundred tons of ice and they crushed that up for slush."

The new snow technique was extremely capable for many reasons: it was quieter, it was more realistic, and it could be controlled more effectively for filming. The white ghostly mists no longer floated aimlessly. The new mixture was odorless, with no ill effects when it landed on clothes, the sets, or paint and wood. Most of all, it did not sting in the eye like flying gypsum. Many actors in the 1930s and '40s detested filming snowy scenes because the gypsum smarted when the flakes landed in their eyes.

The Academy of Motion Picture Arts and Sciences recognized these accomplishments and at the 1948 Oscars, the Academy bestowed a special citation to the RKO special effects team for their "development of a new method of simulating fallen snow."

Life's Wonderful Surprises

BY RAY SAVAGE

I called her Snow. Adriana Caselotti was the singing and speaking voice of Snow White in Walt Disney's 1937 classic film *Snow White and the Seven Dwarfs*. This was Disney's first full-length animated motion picture.

In 1990, new in Hollywood, I was playing the movie's soundtrack in my apartment and listening to Adriana's voice. There is something about her voice that I've loved ever since I was a child. *Snow White* was the first movie I ever saw in a theater, and I still remember how amazing it was. I don't know what prompted me to play the soundtrack, but I began to recall these early memories and Adriana's voice sounded still very much alive. I wondered if she was. I looked at the tape cassette insert to find her name. It was listed: Adriana Caselotti as Snow White. I later learned it was rare to see her name on most recording products produced before 1990. In fact, she's not credited in the film. None of the voice talent got credit. With only her name to go on, I checked the Los Angeles phone book and one Adriana Caselotti was listed. I took a chance and called. Not only was she still alive, she was still Snow White. She spoke and sang exactly as she'd sounded in 1937. That's right, after I explained the nature of my call, how I wished to meet her and get her autograph, she agreed to meet me by singing—over the phone—"Someday My Prince Will Come."

She invited me to drop by in a couple of days for an autograph, but explained that her health wasn't what it once was and that she expected it would only be a fifteen-minute visit. When I got there she offered me a beer within the first five minutes. Fifteen minutes turned into five hours and a few more beers. We hit it off instantly, and my first friend in Hollywood became my best friend for the next seven years.

The first day we met, we talked about everything under the sun. She signed several items for me and gave me an autographed Snow White wall clock. She also invited me to come back later in the week to join her and her friends for dinner. *Wow!* She seemed to like me as much as I liked her. We just clicked. And the surprises began.

I had first seen *It's a Wonderful Life* in 1989 when I bought the video. Friends had been suggesting that I'd really like the film if I saw it. I was immediately a new fan and had a new film to add to my list of favorites. I watched it twice, back to back. I had been writing letters to Jimmy Stewart ever since I was about eleven years old. He'd always reply with a signed photo and a personal note. I had enjoyed so many of his films over the years. Hoping to meet him, I stopped by his home in early 1990, but I was told by his housekeeper that he was out. So as not to bother the great Stewart, I didn't rush back the next day. I waited until the last day of October.

On my way home from my job in Century City (near Beverly Hills), I drove up to Sunset Boulevard in rush hour traffic and I had a thought . . . maybe Halloween would be the one night out of the year he'd be open to an uninvited visitor. So with that in mind, I gave it a go. I wanted to meet George Bailey. I turned onto Roxbury Drive and headed to number 918. In my mind, I was entering Bedford Falls (although Bedford Drive is in fact a few blocks over). Talk about a magical neighborhood. Lucy's house was next door to Stewart's.

I could see a gathering of kids and their parents, all well-wishing trick or treaters. The group stood at Stewart's front door, and there were welcoming lights on throughout the home. Maybe he was home and giving out candy. I parked my car and grabbed a pen and an index card for a possible autograph. It was 5:30 when I got up to the house. The door was closed and the group had left. A security guard was hired to keep an eye on things, and I checked with him first since I had to get past him on the walkway. "Sure he's home, go on up and ring the bell," he said.

My God, here we are, I thought. My heart was

The voice of Walt Disney's Snow White was a young Italian soprano named Adriana Caselotti. Never credited, she can be heard singing in the background at Martini's bar in It's a Wonderful Life.

beating like a giant drum. I rang the bell. That same housekeeper opened the door again. "Sorry, Mr. and Mrs. Stewart just sat down to have dinner. "

Not what I wanted to hear. I asked if I could try a little later because I really wanted to meet him. It was a blatant attempt at stalling to keep her from closing the door. Maybe if I could squeeze just ten more seconds out of the housekeeper, Jimmy might come to the door.

Right as I gave up and said, "Thanks anyway," and the housekeeper began to close the door, I was astonished to see the couple themselves walking side by side toward me. Jimmy was dabbing a napkin at his chin. He looked at me and smiled. Gloria was beaming as if she had overheard my request and encouraged him to greet his fan. "How are you?" he asked, still dabbing at his face with the napkin and swallowing the last bite of his dinner.

I was in complete shock. He

was larger than life—much taller than I'd ever imagined. He wore a warm-looking chestnut brown sweater and motioned for me to enter. As we shook hands I thanked him for all the years of great entertainment, and for always being so kind to answer my letters. He knew my appreciation was sincere and kindly signed my index card. I just wished I had a camera, but I was not as prepared for this as I should have been.

His home was very warm on this chilly October evening. He had a fire burning in the living room. It was so comfortable, I wanted to stay the night. But he had already been so kind to get up from the table, and I didn't want to keep him. We talked a bit, and I explained the I was too old to trick or treat, but I'd wanted to meet him for many years. He laughed, "That's fine. That's fine.

"I'm happy to meet you, too," he said. "Happy Halloween."

I felt bad that I didn't really know what to say to his wife, Gloria, and I made sure to thank her and tell her how much this moment meant to me. She knew. Jimmy did too.

We shook hands once more and I headed for the door and left in a daze, thinking, *I did it! I met George Bailey!*

I couldn't wait to tell my friend Adriana. The next day at her house, she wanted to hear all about it. "Oh, he was great! I remember him. How's he doing? Wow, that's great, you met him!

"You know, I worked in one of his films years ago," she said.

"You did?" I asked.

"Yeah, some silly old Christmas movie when I was doing some extra work in the late forties. But I never saw my scene. They must have cut me out of it."

I asked if the movie was *It's a Wonderful Life.*

"Yeah, that's the one," she said.

"You were in *It's a Wonderful Life?!*" I asked again in amazement.

"Yeah," she told me, "no big deal. I watched the thing twice and never saw myself."

Surprised, I told her it was one of my three all-time favorite films. The other two are *Snow White,* of course, and *The Wizard of Oz.* (I had heard that Snow White's voice was heard during the Tin Man's song, "If I Only Had a Heart." We had talked about this the day we met and she'd confirmed that she was paid $100 to record the "Wherefore Art Thou, Romeo?" line during Jack Haley's solo.)

I said to her, "Snow, those three films are more than just *my* favorites. They are considered to be three of the greatest films ever made. And if we find you in *It's a Wonderful Life,* you are linked to all three of them! No one else can claim that."

She told me to have a look but not to expect much. She remembered bits and pieces of the work she did with Frank Capra and recalled filming a snowy scene on a sidewalk with other extras, where she was singled out to sing a duet with another Italian singer. She remembered the song as an upbeat little Italian tune, but she couldn't remember the other singer's name. She also remembered a line that she said to Jimmy Stewart on camera, "Don't forget, George, I'm your cousin!" And that was about all she recalled from her day on the set in Encino.

That night, I watched the film carefully, rewinding different parts and looking again and again. Nothing. I decided to watch it all over again like the first time I had seen it, but I still couldn't find her. I watched everything. That was my mistake.

When Adriana asked if I saw anything, I had to tell her "Not yet . . . but I'm going to keep looking." "No," she said, "don't waste your time. . . . I looked at the film twice myself and they must've cut me out. They do that."

I told her that I never tire of watching *It's a Wonderful Life,* so it was no problem to keep an open eye. I think we were both optimistic.

Almost seven years passed.

Adriana had now turned eighty and was falling ill. She had cancer. We talked a lot these final days, between hospital visits and my spending the night when she didn't want to be alone. She had no complaints and was completely fulfilled with the wonderful life she had lived, and she was very proud to have been Snow White—especially when the film was finally released on video and Disney finally recognized her as the legend she was. Johnny Carson even had her as a guest on the *Tonight Show,* which was one of her favorite moments in life.

She didn't want to leave this world just yet, but at the same time she was very curious about the next one, and she missed many of her friends and loved ones who had already passed on. "I'm not trying to be morbid," she'd say, "but I'm kind of looking forward to the experience that is such a mystery." She knew, from dreams she'd been having, that many people she had known were awaiting her arrival. She was very curious, but I know she would have stayed with us a while longer given the

chance. She joked that Walt wanted to do *Snow White II.* She loved life and all her fans around the world, and she was getting more attention from people now in the 1990s than she did in 1937 when *Snow White* premiered. But she knew it was her time.

One night in late December 1996, I was home in my apartment in Beachwood Canyon, up in the hills of Hollywood, directly under the famous sign. I was preparing to go up north for Christmas to be with my family and friends, wrapping some gifts and watching that "silly old Christmas movie" for the umpteenth time. I'd occasionally look up from wrapping a gift to watch a scene, keeping an open eye for Adriana. That was my mistake from the start. I was only watching with my eyes, and not my ears.

I walked into the kitchen with my buddy Winston, the big orange cat, and was just listening to the film. The television was connected to several speakers throughout my apartment, and it was from the kitchen speaker that I heard Adriana's voice. I thought I was hearing things because it sounded like Adriana was in my apartment. After seven years of friendship, there was no mistaking her voice. All that she had told me of what she remembered about her work in the film flashed through my mind. It was a duet I was hearing, and it was in Italian, but it wasn't during any outdoor snow scene, it was placed inside Martini's bar behind George Bailey's drinking, weeping, and praying—arguably, the most memorable scene in the film.

I rushed into the living room and saw the classic scene. I could hear Adriana's voice in the background, but she was not in sight. When George Bailey is punched in the face by Mr. Welch, her singing stops instantly. The song ends and she starts up with a slow song for a few more seconds. I rewound the tape to the establishing bar shot and Adriana's voice sang on cue. Then I saw her. For seven seconds. Just behind Stewart, she wears a single flower in her hair, earrings and necklaces, and a long-sleeved white blouse. She is seen chatting with an unseen person. She disappears when the camera zooms into a tight crop of Stewart as he takes the glass from his lips and sets it on the bar. Her singing voice continues in the background. Bailey glances at his only remaining self-worth—a life insurance policy—and then he begins to pray to God. Adriana sings behind the entire prayer scene.

After nearly seven years of searching for Adriana, she found me when I wasn't even looking.

As much as I wanted to, it was too late in the evening to call Adriana because of her condition. She was sleeping a lot now. The next morning I gave her a call and told her what I had found, and she said "Bring it over, bring it over." I had the scene all cued up and ready to go.

Adriana was in her bedroom, laid up in her bed, and was being cared for under a hospice program. She was awake and alert and eager to see what I had found. I popped in the video and the scene came on. She smiled. Then she smiled more. Then she began to sing in Italian along with it. She knew it. I looked at her and said, "That's you, isn't it?" Looking me straight back in the eye she barked back, "Who *else* would it be?" She was as stunned as I was. Adriana told me all about the song she was singing, an old Italian song called "Vieni, Vieni." We looked and listened dozens of times. As quickly as it flashed by, Adriana was so surprised to see herself in the background. She loved it. She explained that Capra must have taken the duet she recorded in the street scene and dubbed it into Martini's bar instead.

I only stayed for an hour this time, and it would be one of our last visits. I left the video at her bedside. Adriana passed away shortly after the new year of 1997, but not before she found the missing link—just one more of life's wonderful surprises. "Wouldn't you know it, after half a century the mystery is finally solved. And you solved it, Ray!" Snow said. *Snow White and the Seven Dwarfs. The Wizard of Oz. It's a Wonderful Life.* Three of the greatest films Hollywood ever produced, and my dear friend Snow was a part of all three. It's truly gratifying to know that I discovered Adriana's connection to Capra's master-piece and was able to share it with her, and now with you.

Don't blink: Adriana Caselotti can be seen briefly in the background, just over Jimmy Stewart's shoulder. Caselotti's unmistakable soprano vocals are also heard briefly during the scene in two songs, "Vieni, Vieni" and "Santa Lucia."

2

ᴌife's Memories

JIMMY STEWART, in an interview with film historian Leonard Maltin, fondly recalled working with Henry Travers, the puffy-faced actor who played Clarence, his character's guardian angel:

Henry! Of course, he was just exactly right, just exactly right for Clarence. And this was another quality Frank [Capra] had. He just hits the right note as far as casting is concerned. There couldn't have been anybody better than Henry Travers for Clarence, there just couldn't. His timing and his looks and the way he played it straight. You could see him absolutely guarding himself against anything that would be a comic-strip type of thing. Because he was an angel. He didn't have any wings, but he was an angel. It was fascinating. It was just a joy to see him work and to work with him. In that scene where we're drying off after being in the water, I kept hearing these things that he was saying. Frank had said, "Let's not rehearse it. Let's keep it natural. Just go ahead with it and we'll see how it plays, but do the whole darn thing no matter what." We did, and I was just fascinated with that man. His timing, and always putting the humor where it belonged. Looking up every once in a

An eager Clarence is near the end of his quest to earn his wings.

while when I talked, and then, when I said that I wished I'd never been born . . . the way he did it. The take wasn't fake, but it—you know, it was just sort of amazed. He fascinated me.

Donna Reed, in 1975, reflected on her portrayal of Mary Hatch:

It was the best of times—inspired, extemporaneous, fun, hard work, and especially memorable for me. The great Capra was working with his sure and pure instinct for the human qualities—goodness, badness, courage, despair (love and death, with no fear of looking hard at the latter), especially as they are borne by the common man, our everyday kind of neighbor.

Capra loved his "neighbor" passionately and presented that good man with dogged determination to make him "big." There were no tricky camera angles or setups to hamper, restrict, or manipulate the always larger picture—the character on Capra's film.

I remember working harder for Capra than any other director before or after, for a deceptively simple, uncomplicated small-town

And they were gonna shoot the works.

Donna Reed (real name: Donna Mullenger) was twenty-five when she portrayed Mary Bailey.

"girl and woman" character. I did things I had never done before—danced the Charleston a little, sang a little, fell over backward in a swimming pool (ending up by using a double because I saw very little), played light comedy as well as drama, aged from eighteen to forty years—and he made it all look so simple and easy on screen.

That's the trick of film acting—it must always look simple and easy, even if you've nearly killed yourself doing it.

We made *It's a Wonderful Life* in less than three months. It was such a brief encounter that now, looking back thirty years, it seems amazing that in so short a time we created such a remarkably moving film—thanks mostly to the wonderfully gifted Frank Capra!

(REPRINTED BY PERMISSION OF VICTOR SCHERLE AND
WILLIAM TURNER LEVY, AUTHORS OF *THE FILMS OF FRANK CAPRA*)

FRANK CAPRA revealed how he handled some of the film's most difficult scenes:

For a long time we were worried about how to show heaven. How are we going to film it? Heaven is never the same to any two people. My heaven wouldn't be your heaven. So, it just became ridiculous. I knew we wouldn't please everybody, and I knew we'd probably get some laughs with the thing that we naturally didn't want. So rather than getting laughs that we didn't want, I used laughs we did want. In dealing with heaven, I did it with a humorous way. This little method of doing it with the stars and little cartoons and such came up after many sessions in which we tried to figure out how to shoot this scene between these angels and this little angel. You see, after he came down, you accepted him as something incarnate, he drew flesh when he came down. But up there, how do you show him?

This was, in a way, a way out of a difficulty. But a conscious way. And when a thing gets tough, try to make it funny and it'll go over. It's like Mae West with her sex. If you make it funny, you can get away with murder. So heaven was humorous this way and it didn't offend anybody.

I suppose the most difficult scene, and I think one of the best scenes in the picture, is the little scene where he comes in and raises hell with his kids, just before he runs out and tries to throw himself in the river. That whole scene with the kid playing the piano. It's a very dramatic scene, and yet, it can get laughs. That little girl there pounding on that piano is funny and that little kid asking those silly questions is funny. Here you're playing with dynamite, you're playing with laughs in a dramatic scene. Which do you want it to do? That was one of the most difficult to stage because if it becomes too

This is one of the most realistic and effective scenes of holiday desperation ever filmed. Stewart's acting is masterful here as he gets caught in a downward spiral.

funny, the drama will not come over and they'd laugh at the drama too. And audiences will think they have to laugh at everything.

SHELDON LEONARD remembered his role as Nick the bartender:

It gave me a kind of immortality that I never expected. Fifty years ago. I had converted from the acting trade. I was then busily involved in directing. But my friend Frank Capra asked me to play Nick the Bartender in this and I could not resist the opportunity to work with that very talented man.

My part was all of about four memorable days. There was an inherent challenge in playing Nick the bartender because it wasn't just one character, it was two characters. The before and after character. There was the agreeable, smiling, pleasant man in the early part of the picture and the monster in the second part. As an actor it was challenging and yet very rewarding to be able to make it come off under Capra's talented direction.

Nick doesn't want any characters around to give the place atmosphere.

Nick (Sheldon Leonard) gets ready to toss out Mr. Welch (Stanley Andrews), the man who popped George in the face.

Baileys' Housewarming Toast

Bread! That this house may never know hunger. *Salt!* That life may always have flavor. *And wine!* That joy and prosperity may reign forever. Enter the (homeowner) castle!

Martini's no more live in Potter's Field. They loaded up the truck and they moved to Bailey . . . Park that is.

TODD KARNS explained how he got the role of war hero Harry Bailey:

Well, my father was a rather well known character actor in Hollywood. His name was Roscoe Karns. I had met Donna Reed before the war at MGM. She was very pretty. She was a very professional, mature, giving actress. After the war, I had to gear up my career, as all other actors did too. I got an audition to read for Mr. Capra and I guess he saw something. I was signed under an exclusive contract by Liberty Films. There were going to be four films a year, but then there was a bit of a recession. Television was rearing its ugly head and so the company went belly up after one year.

"A toast: To my big brother George—the richest man in town."

We were on location at Beverly Hills High, my alma mater. They'd built the pool the year after I graduated. The gym floor would open up, revealing a swimming pool. There were about a hundred and fifty kids, dancing, screaming. I tried to do the Charleston, but I never learned. Actually, a few of the kids dove into the pool.

KAROLYN GRIMES, who will forever be known as Zuzu, admits that her primary memories from working on the film were not those alongside Jimmy Stewart:

I was only six at the time. This may sound really dumb, but I liked the sets because they were make-believe, and when I was a little girl I liked to make-believe. The outside of the walls of the house, there was that foamite stuff outside all over the bushes underneath the windowsills. I can just see it. It was the first time I'd ever seen snow in my life. Everything is artificial. I remember the smell of that, I loved the smell. And I remember looking in the windows with the lights on in the windows, peeking in the windows and just watch-

"Look, daddy . . . paste it." Watch this charming scene closely: George secretly hides the fallen rose petals in his watch pocket. Zuzu clearly observes him concealing the petals and not really repairing the flower at all—and yet, she's content just the same. Now that's a sweet kid.

ing. I really liked that more than anything else. I've never told anybody that. Yeah, because it was make-believe. It was like looking into somebody else's life. All the people were running back and forth and getting the cameras ready and the lights done and I loved the hubbub that went along with all of that. And the big fans blowing the snow.

The set was like three walls, like a shell. All of that was pretty fascinating. I just liked being on the set. I always had this super big curiosity. Like when I was in the film *Rio Grande*, with John Wayne, and they had brought Indians off the reservation in. And we were told without any hesitation that we were to stay away from those Indians. Never were we to go around the Indians. Of course, I was constantly peeking and lurking around and watching the Indians.

I also vividly remember Jimmy Hawkins' mother kitting a brown dress. Knitted dresses were very popular back then and she was using this big round needle, sitting in a chair off on the corner of the set. I couldn't take my eyes off of it. I don't like that color. I don't like it now and I didn't like it then. Later on, many years later, when we were brought together I asked Jimmy if his mother still knitted and he said, "Yes, she does . . . I can't believe you remember that."

CHARLES LANE, who portrayed Potter's rent collector in one brief scene, went on to become one of motion picture and television's most prolific character actors. He remembers his long association with Frank Capra:

What did I like best? That's pretty easy—my relationship with Capra and the pictures that I did. I did a lot of them. When you get into films, I'm very prejudiced: I think he was the biggest talent we ever had. He used the same people over and over again, in different roles, naturally in different pictures. My relationship with Capra was more on a personal level, that's why I admired him so much. He had an ability to relate to human beings.

I've seen *It's a Wonderful Life.* Not long ago I watched it again. I think it's a little old fashioned. They're all old fashioned . . . and they should be. Jim [Stewart] said it was his favorite. I really don't know why. Because I think some of the other things he did—for me, anyway—were better. But as a rule, I can't stand to watch myself. If I'm on television, I don't watch. I think most of us are that way, or we used to be anyway. Maybe sometimes the director would ask you to go in and watch the dailies. I could never go and watch dailies. That would drive me crazy. You'd sit there and say, "Why did I read that line like that . . . my God!" All you do is bellyache at what you didn't do, what you should've done. But it's too late. One day too late.

I rarely had any regrets with Frank Capra and the work I did with him. You see, I lived through a period here in town where in order to direct a picture, you had to be some kind of a foreigner. And they imported all these Prussian and Polish directors. They were all bastards. And on top of that, they weren't any good. And we went through a terrible period of being persecuted by these guys. So when you came around with somebody like Howard Hawkes or Frank Capra and some of the other marvelous directors we had, you wanted to do your best. Frank was tickled because I

Mr. Potter's rent collector (Charles Lane) warns, "one of these days, this bright young man is going to be asking George Bailey for a job."

Spelling Bee

Okay, okay . . . so Tommy Bailey didn't know how to spell. Admit it, the words he asked about were toughies:

frank·in·cense (frang'kin-sens) *n.* a fragrant and aromatic gum resin from African and Asian trees of a genus (Boswellia of the family Burseraceae) of Somalia and southern coastal Arabia that is an important incense resin and was used in ancient times in religious rites and in embalming and in perfumes.

hal·le·lu·jah (hal' e-loo'ye) *interj.* Word used to express praise, joy, or thanks. 1. An exclamation of "hallelujah." 2. A music composition expressing praise and based on the word "hallelujah." [Heb. hallelûyah.]

worked for him a lot and I was very fond of him. Frank was not like the temperamental directors, and as a result of that, he got much more out of you. He got everything out of you. He wasn't mellow. He was a little tough dago, you know, he could get sore. I don't know, he had an approach right from the casting, that gave you the feeling that you were there because he thought you were the best person in town to do it. And that gave you that marvelous security on the set, because lots of times, you go on the set—actors do—and they're so terrified that they're not gonna work out. Particularly when you're young, you're scared.

ELLEN CORBY, forever known as TV's Grandma Walton, recalled in 1974 her memorable role as the meek Miss Davis, the bank customer who only wished to withdraw $17.50 to get by:

I think Frank Capra was the first person to prove to me that there was no such thing as a small part. In *It's a Wonderful Life* I had only one line, and for that I received not only some nice compliments, but a kiss from Jimmy Stewart. (A piece of business that wasn't in the script!) Matter of fact, I'm not sure the dialogue was in the script—but Mr. Capra's mind seemed to be channeled into that great creative source. He didn't just shoot what was on paper; he continued to create on the set.

Twelve-year-old Larry Simms, who became famous as "Baby Dumpling" in twenty-six Blondie movies, handled the role of the oldest Bailey child like a pro. So much was said with just this quiet expression.

Clarence's Mulled Wine

Here's a lively recipe for mulled wine, just like Clarence ordered from Nick the bartender. What is mulled wine, you ask? Mulled wine is simply heated and spiced wine, and the traditional beverage has a long history of consumption during holidays and the colder months. It's sometimes prepared with honey, cinnamon, fruit, or cardamom. Here's one such recipe you may enjoy trying this holiday season.

2¼ cups water
2 tablespoons sugar
3 whole cinnamon sticks
2 bottles red wine
1 clove
½ cup cognac
  Lemon twists (optional)

In a large saucepan bring the water, cinnamon, clove, and sugar to a boil. Add the wine, then heat slowly until hot again. Stir in the cognac, and remove from the heat. Pour into festive mugs and add a lemon twist to each, if you prefer.

It's a Wonderful Life was one of the first pictures I did when I went into acting after eleven years as a script supervisor. Fifty percent of me was still working behind the camera, and I was keenly interested in everything Mr. Capra did. He was head and shoulders above most of the directors I had worked with. He was quiet and inspiring. I wanted to please him more than anything else in the world. He didn't need noise to be forceful, and I loved the way he delegated the work so that assistant director Art Black and others made the noise and Mr. Capra watched the results with a twinkle, as though Art and the others were being naughty!

JIMMY HAWKINS, *the youngest member of the cast, commented on his role of little Tommy Bailey in his* It's a Wonderful Life Trivia Book *(written with Paul Petersen):*

It was the week of June 13, 1946 . . . right after the war, and people were just getting back to normal. I was a child actor, four and a half

Emmy Award–winning character actress Ellen Corby, known to television audiences as Grandma Walton *(left)*, portrayed meek Mrs. Davis, who in a brief but memorable scene asks to withdraw just $17.50 to get by.

years old, going to be five in November. That one-half year was a big deal at the time. . . .

I remember my mom would wake me up real early . . . it was still dark outside. We'd take the bus, then transfer to a streetcar a couple of times (the Red Cars were still operating then). I remember waiting for the streetcar while shop owners were opening for the day. We'd arrive at our destination, the RKO-Pathé Studios in Culver City, right down the street from MGM. (We used to refer to it as M-Jim, 'cause I'd already done a lot of movies there.)

We went to Stage 14. When I walked onto the stage, going through the two big doors separated by a little anteroom (and the

doors were too big for me to pull open), I can recall the odor. Old soundstages have a peculiar smell. I can only describe it as a cookie smell. I remember that scent, and I remember the nice memory it brings back.

It took two weeks to film all the stuff with the kids. I remember Frank Capra getting down in almost a sitting position, a squat really, to discuss with me, eye to eye, what it was he wanted me to do. . . .

I remember one scene in particular with Jimmy Stewart where I'm putting tinsel on his head and all of a sudden he grabs me and pulls me into his cheek. We rehearsed this a few times and then did a couple of takes. I was wearing this Santa Claus mask around my neck and every time Mr. Stewart would pull me to him the rough inside of the mask would scratch my face. I sure didn't like that feeling but I knew enough not to flinch on film.

"'Scuse me . . . 'Scuse me." Jimmy Hawkins was four and a half years old when he played little Tommy Bailey, the tot who burped.

VIRGINIA PATTON MOSS *recalls her great concern for an unusual detail she had to deal with during production:*

In the film, where I was introduced as Ruth Dakin Bailey, you know, Mrs. Harry Bailey, Stewart's sister in law, the scene was shot very early in the morning at the Pasadena train station. I descended the

Johnny Carson hosted a television special about the extraordinary life of Jimmy Stewart. Near the end of the 1987 retrospective, Carson asked his friend how he'd like to be remembered. Stewart sweetly stammered for a moment and answered, "I'd say, a guy that believed in hard work, and decent values, love of country, love of family, love of community, and love of God."

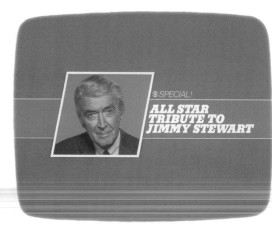

Donna Reed's sparkling performance as Mary Bailey won acclaim, but it was her role in *From Here to Eternity* (1953) that earned her an Academy Award. Reed died at age sixty-four in 1986; her wish was that her Oscar be displayed in her hometown of Denison, Iowa.

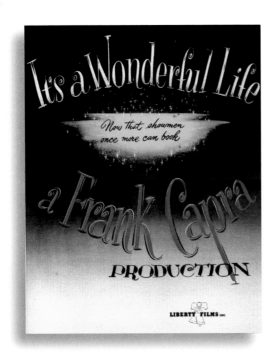

FIFTEEN CENTS

August 8, 1938

TIME

The Weekly Newsmagazine

Color Photograph for Time by Paul Dorsey

Volume XXXII

DIRECTOR FRANK CAPRA
His stories cannot match his story.
(See CINEMA)

Number 6

Circulation Office, 350 East 22nd Street, Chicago.   (Reg. U. S. Pat. Off.)   Editorial and Advertising Offices, Time & Life Building, Rockefeller Center, New York, N. Y.

★ ★ ★ ★ ★

DECEMBER 30, 1946   15c

Newsweek

THE MAGAZINE OF NEWS SIGNIFICANCE

The Return of Jimmy Stewart
(See 'Movies')

Actor Todd Karns (Harry Bailey) was an accomplished painter. This piece, depicting a moment from *It's a Wonderful Life,* was one of his favorites and the actor reprinted the image on cards for fans.

"It's a Wonderful Life" in Bedford Falls

Above: The Bailey kids, all grown up, posed together for the first time in nearly fifty years when they reunited as part of a special holiday promotion sponsored by Target stores in 1993. *L-R:* Jimmy Hawkins (Tommy), Carol Coombs (Janie), Karolyn Grimes (Zuzu), and Larry Simms (Peter). *Below:* Some of the surviving cast members were reunited in Jimmy Stewart's hometown of Indiana, Pennsylvania, in 1996. *L-R:* Bob Anderson (young George), Argentina Brunetti (Mrs. Martini), Todd Karns (Harry Bailey), Carol Coombs (Janie), and Karolyn Grimes (Zuzu).

Clockwise from top left: Virginia Patton (Ruth Dakin Bailey) and, of course, Santa Claus were the guests of honor at a holiday charity ball in 2002. Karolyn Grimes reunited with Jimmy Stewart in New York in 1990. Sheldon Leonard (Nick the bartender), at age eighty-seven, posed at the bar of his Beverly Hills home, where his Emmy Awards and accolades from a long career were displayed (1995). Prolific character actor Charles Lane (Potter's rent collector), in his nineties.

This Week
MAGAZINE

Des Moines Sunday Register
MAGAZINE SECTION · DECEMBER 15 1946

STEWART'S STORY: HE COMES HOME SEE PAGE 18

THOSE CHRISTMAS TIES!
by Charles D. Rice and Ken Jones
...Page 4

Ann and Henry Travers in the backyard garden of their Hollywood home (1961).

train steps, and what a thrill to be welcomed to "Bedford Falls" with Jimmy's kiss!

Later the buttered popcorn concerned me quite a bit though. As a new bride, traveling to be introduced to my new in-laws, I was dressed in hat, heels, suit, and white gloves. In the following scene, Mr. Capra directed us to walk to a popcorn stand and nibble on buttered popcorn.

What about the gloves? Do I eat the buttered morsels with my gloves on? Take them off? The camera did pull in for a closeup of our heads, not my hands in butter-covered white gloves.

I treasure my memories of my time with Jimmy Stewart and Frank Capra. Jimmy was such a natural, the very same off the screen as he was before the cameras. And Mr. Capra was a very talented, gifted, kind, sympathetic person, an artist in every sense of the word.

"Ruth Dakin Bailey, if you don't mind." Harry's new bride (Virginia Patton) is introduced during this scene filmed at the Pasadena, California, train station. "And Jimmy Stewart kissed me!" brags the actress still today.

The Beloved Mother—Beulah Bondi

BY PHIL POTEMPA

Beulah Bondi's favorite advice to young actors and actresses usually included the phrase "age is just a number." During a career spanning more than sixty years, Bondi never wanted to be remembered for just one role. But in her later years Bondi admitted that her string of performances as Jimmy Stewart's mother ranked among her favorites.

In 1939, she played Mrs. Smith in Frank Capra's *Mr. Smith Goes to Washington.* "I had to do very little in that movie, other than look concerned, which I think I did very well," Bondi said in a 1980 interview with her hometown newspaper, the *Vidette-Messenger.* Five years later, Capra brought her back as the object of Stewart's maternal affections in *It's a Wonderful Life* and gave her greater flexibility to showcase her talents.

"In *It's a Wonderful Life,* I was given a much greater opportunity to display acting range, by playing both George Bailey's lov-

RICHARD GOODSON COLLECTION

Beulah Bondi as Ma Bailey.

ing mother and also the woman she might have been had he not been born," Bondi said. "It's the movie remembered by so many, because it touched so many hearts."

Bondi's last turn as Stewart's mom came in the fall of 1971, on *The Jimmy Stewart Show* on CBS in an episode titled "The Identity Crisis."

Born in Chicago May 3, 1888 (some sources say 1892), at age three Bondi moved with her parents, Abraham and Eva Bondy, to Valparaiso, Indiana. Once Bondi and her older brother were in school, her mother returned to college to receive a Bachelor of Arts in theater arts and began teaching acting classes. Bondi said some of her earliest memories of "play acting" was when her mother would teach her to "recite" just before bedtime.

The Bondys lived at 203 N. Washington Street in Valparaiso, just a few blocks from the downtown courthouse square. She made her theatrical acting debut at age nine at Valparaiso's Memorial Opera House, in the title role in a touring production of *Little Lord Fauntleroy.*

"The child actor that was supposed to play the lead had become ill, and so mother got me the part," Bondi said in a 1972 interview with Camilla Snyder for the *San Francisco Herald-Examiner.* "With mother's help, I learned the forty-seven-page part. By the night the play opened, I not only knew all of my lines, but I was prompting anyone who wasn't up on their lines too." Bondi said the experience of playing "that little boy role" helped turn her into a "character actress." While attending Valparaiso University, Bondi played a debutante in the school production of *An American Citizen,* and she also provided a published prediction about herself and her classmates in the school yearbook, *The Record.* Known as "the class poet," Bondi wrote a parody of classical verse titled *The Beneficences,* in which she attributed one of the nine muses to each of the nine oratory graduates of her 1916 senior classes. Prophetically, she assigned Urania, the muse of astronomy, to herself, so she might "one day be among the stars." Bondi received her bachelor's degree in 1916, and a master's degree in 1918, both in Oratory and both from Valparaiso.

Following commencement, she went to Indianapolis, where she was signed by Stuart Walker, the head of one of the best known American repertory companies at the time. She stayed with the company for two years before leaving to tour in summer stock and eventually arriving in New York. In 1919 the twenty-seven-year-old Bondi played a seventy-year-old servant in her first Off-Broadway role, beginning what would be a

trademark for the actress of playing characters twice her age—or older. She landed her first major Broadway role in 1929 as elderly tenement landlady Emma Jones in Elmer Rice's Pulitzer Prize–winning drama *Street Scene.*

After a short stint in 1930 in New York in the play *Milestones,* she was contracted in 1931 by United Artists to recreate her stage role in the film version of *Street Scene* for Sam Goldwyn. However, she refused to sign what she described as "one of Goldwyn's tricky seven year contracts."

"I was very new to the film medium," she said. "I was fortunate that my introduction to pictures was easy because I was so familiar with my role, but the microphone was completely new to me, as was the limitation of movement. I didn't know anything about lenses or a medium close-up or a long shot. But I was interested enough in movies to want to learn quickly." Bondi told Valparaiso University professor Richard Lee in 1976 during the campus' "Beulah Bondi Days" that she felt her decision to "tear up a contract from Sam Goldwyn" saved her from being "miscast" as a young actress and gave her the advantage of selecting her own roles while other actresses were "forced to take certain parts," a dangerous fate of many contract players of the day.

By 1932, Bondi had completed her third film, *Rain,* co-starring Joan Crawford and Walter Huston. Bondi was already making $500 a week, twenty times more than the salary she had earned on the Indianapolis stage just three years earlier. It was at this time that Bondi chose to change her last name from Bondy to Bondi. According to the late Allegra Nesbit of Valparaiso, a

George Bailey tells his father that he can't bear the thought of being trapped in an office for the rest of his life.

hometown friend of the actress quoted in Bondi's 1981 newspaper obituary in the *Vidette-Messenger,* "Beulah changed her name because she thought the 'i' made it more 'stagey' and it allowed all of the letters to fit above the line on theater marquees. And that name change was done with her family's sanctions." Miss Nesbit, who said she was "like a little sister to Beulah," also said Bondi used her "hazy age" as an advantage throughout her career.

"At the time of her death, all of the newspapers, like the *L.A. Times,* said Beulah was ninety-two. But she was really ninety. Beulah once told me that 'whether it's on stage, on screen, or in life, it's always good to keep others guessing your age.' And that's just want she did 'til the very end," Nesbit said.

Over the years, Bondi starred with a Who's Who of Hollywood. In 1934, she starred with Greta Garbo in *The Painted Veil.* In 1935, she could be seen in theaters acting alongside Margaret Sullivan, Frank

Morgan, Alan Hale, and Cesar Romero in *The Good Fairy.* In 1936, she starred with horror greats Boris Karloff and Bela Lugosi in *The Invisible Ray* and with Marion Davies, Dick Powell, Claude Rains, and Arthur Treacher in *Hearts Divided.* In that same year, Bondi was honored when the Motion Picture Arts Academy added a new category, "best supporting actress," and she was nominated for the Oscar for her role in *The Gorgeous Hussy,* also starring Jimmy Stewart, Joan Crawford, Robert Taylor, Franchot Tone, and Lionel Barrymore as President Andrew Jackson. Gale Sondergaard won instead, for her film debut in *Anthony Adverse.*

In 1938, Bondi co-starred with Jimmy Stewart in the comedy *Vivacious Lady,* which also starred Ginger Rogers. That year, she was again nominated for the best supporting actress Oscar for her performance as Mary Wilkins in *Of Human Hearts.* Her fellow nominees included Billie Burke and Spring Byington, who was nominated for *You Can't*

Take It With You, which took home best picture and best director for Frank Capra. But Bondi was beat out for the Oscar by Fay Bainter for her role as the housekeeper in *Jezebel,* which also netted the best actress Oscar for Bette Davis.

Bondi said she never felt any regrets about not winning an Oscar, but she admitted "feeling badly" for losing a role she truly coveted that same year. In 1938, she was selected to play the role of Aunt Polly in *The Adventures of Tom Sawyer* after the first choice, actress May Robson, became ill. But when Robson recovered sooner than expected, Bondi was let out of the contract and the scenes were all reshot. Her other admitted disappointment was when she was told she had the lead role of Ma Joad in *The Grapes of Wrath,* only to learn later it was given to Jane Darwell, who won an Oscar for the performance. Over the course of

the sixty-five major motion pictures Bondi appeared in, she marveled at the many friends she made who became "like family," since she never married or had children of her own. For example, actress Ellen Corby remained a close friend and often joked how she played the same role originated by Bondi in the 1934 film *The Painted Veil* when it was remade in 1957 as *The Seventh Sin.* The two actresses would again share similar roles on the television series *The Waltons.*

Bondi's last three films were 1962's *The Wonderful World of the Brothers Grimm,* in which she played a gypsy, *Tammy, Tell Me True* in 1961, and *Tammy and the Doctor* in 1963. During the 1960s and 1970s, all of Bondi's roles were in television. For example, at age eighty-five, she played a guest spot in 1974 on the short-lived CBS western series *Dirty Sally* starring Jeannette Nolan and Dack Rambo, as a woman

Throughout her career gentle Beulah Bondi portrayed Jimmy Stewart's mother five times, most memorably as Ma Bailey.

Beulah Bondi happily clutches her Emmy Award for playing Martha Corrine on The Waltons.

film she "wasn't sorry she had turned it down." Ironically, she had a change of heart and three years later agreed to play Grandpa Walton's elderly "mountain woman" sister-in-law, Martha Corrine, in the September 12, 1974, two-hour episode opening the series' third season. Bondi's character was fighting a government eviction from her land, which was marked for development. And in an episode two seasons later titled "The Pony Cart," which aired December 2, 1976, Bondi once again played the ninety-year-old, who at first irritates the family with her meddling and later reaffirms the meaning of "family ties" to the Waltons. When the Emmy nominations were announced in April 1977, the nominees for best single performance by an actress in a drama or limited series were Madge Sinclair for an episode of *Roots*, Kim Hunter for *Baretta* and Jessica Walter for *The Streets of San Francisco*. A very public rift between the National Academy of Television Arts and Sciences and Hollywood industry insiders caused the original slate of nominees to be scrapped. New nominations were announced in early August 1977. While Sinclair and Walter were retained on the ballot, Susan Blakely was added for *Rich Man, Poor Man II* and Leslie Uggams for *Roots*. Also on the ballot was an elderly but familiar face to many: Beulah Bondi for her *Waltons* episode, "The Pony Cart." Though Uggams was the predicted winner, it was Bondi who slowly made her way to the stage to accept the statuette on September

preparing to die but wanting to see her grandson return from military service.

In a 1978 interview with the *Vidette-Messenger*, Bondi said she was offered the grandmother role in the 1971 television movie *The Homecoming*, which led to the popular CBS series *The Waltons*, starring her friend Ellen Corby in the role she had turned down. After reading the script, Bondi said she "didn't particularly care for the part" and after watching the completed

11, 1977, as the theme from *The Waltons* played in the background. She said that for the first time in her life she was finally cast to play a character her actual age, and it won her worthy praise.

"My, isn't this beautiful," she said at the podium as she grasped her Emmy. "This is truly a bonus." She also thanked the Academy (which in earlier years had honored her contemporaries Marion Lorne, Alice Pearce, and David Burns posthumously) for recognizing her while she was "still alive." Bondi last visited her hometown of Valparaiso in 1978 to receive an honorary Doctorate of Laws degree. That same year, she appeared at the American Film Institute's tribute to Jimmy Stewart, or as she called him, "my most famous screen son."

Bondi lived at the top of a very steep but magnificent hill in Hollywood in a vast, four-level Spanish home, filled with books, that she purchased in 1944. Even in her late eighties, she continued to drive her 1958 Mercedes to the grocery store and do her own shopping. During her later years, she would complain that the only way to reach her home was to travel up the steep incline of Western Avenue, which by then was littered with what she called a "blight of sex shops and massage parlors, all too evident." "We all know what life is, but it is too awful to advertise it in that way," she said in a 1977 newspaper interview. "I feel the same way about the many films today. It isn't just the nudity in pictures I abhor, but the action that is suggested. I went to two controversial films recently, *Last Tango* and *Sunday, Bloody Sunday,* and I found them very offensive. I go to films to learn. Good acting, good writing, good directing, all the techni-

cal part is what I learn from. I'm not squeamish; it's just I don't yearn for the other."

Bondi, whose hobby was traveling the world, including two trips to China, five to Africa, and jaunts to Alaska, liked to share with reporters and students what she considered the most "risque scene" of her filmography, which was with Lionel Barrymore in the 1930s. "I was filming *Gorgeous Hussy* with Barrymore and Joan Crawford, and my mother was coming to see me and visit her first Hollywood film set. She found me having to get in this huge double bed with Lionel in this one scene. She didn't say anything, but she was very surprised, I think. That was 1936, and it was the last time a double bed was allowed in a film for quite a few years. We all laughed at that rule. Now, in films, they can do anything in bed!"

Bondi also explained the importance of being a character actress in a 1980 interview with writer Anthony Slide. "We, the character actresses, are sort of the mortar between the bricks," Bondi said. "I never had any idea of stealing a scene or being better than anyone else. The idea is to make the whole thing look perfect with cooperation." Beulah Bondi was hospitalized early in 1981, following a fall at her home which resulted in several broken ribs. She died on January 11, 1981, at Hollywood's Motion Picture and Television Home and Hospital, with the cause of death listed as pulmonary complications. Under Bondi's photograph in the 1914 Valparaiso University yearbook are the words: "In talent this lady did stand far above, But ever herself we always did love."

The Man in the Wheelchair

Once in a while I get to thinking I'm not so bad. In fact, I begin to think I'm pretty darn good. Then I go charging into a scene with Barrymore, get my ears pinned back, the scene stolen right out of my hand. Then I wonder if, in arguing that I'll be a whiz of an actor by eighty, if I'm giving myself enough time.

JIMMY STEWART, THIS WEEK, DECEMBER 15, 1946

Twelve-year-old Bobbie Anderson was the clean-cut kid who portrayed young George Bailey in the movie's early dramatic scenes, most memorably the one with a drunken Mr. Gower smacking him and injuring his ear. Today, Anderson looks at the film and is quite satisfied with his performance back then. Stewart would later commend him for his performance as the young George Bailey.

Capra must've found that quiet, gentle quality in young Anderson, because he took the time to help cast the film, right down to the extras, and he was confident in his choice for young George.

Anderson, now in his late 60s, says that when Capra selected him, he was already a cool, hard-working, "good little actor," having worked in a few films alongside Shirley Temple and Jackie Cooper. He recalls the first reading with the cast in Capra's office, "around a big dining room table," he says. "He treated me like a professional. He had control on the picture, there was little nonsense, but that's not to say it wasn't fun.

"I called him Frank," says Anderson. "You were one on one with him. I don't recall any intimidation at all." Not with Capra, anyway. Thomas Mitchell was another story. It's hard to imagine silly old Uncle Billy as gruff.

"Thomas Mitchell, well, one day he was getting pretty irritated and I was missing my cues," Anderson explains. "People always say what a great guy Mitchell was. I don't know what he was like personally, but on that day he was a monster. And Lionel Barrymore—you hear these stories of this wheelchaired son of a bitch—he was a sweet man. He grabbed Mitchell by the arm and said, 'I don't think we have to be quite so strong with the lad.'"

There was an intangible aura that went along with the legendary name of Barrymore; the aging actor actually did use a wheelchair and crutches to get around. His hands were wracked with rheumatoid arthritis. "He was confined to his wheelchair as far as I knew," Anderson says, "and his hands were big. His knuckles looked like they were broken. They were huge."

"He would wheel himself to the set and you knew the bull was over," he says. "It was not because he felt he was a big star. He was so professional it made everyone around him stay on their toes. He didn't have to turn a script page. He didn't have to say, 'Where are we today?' He was there, on the set, ready to work and get it over with, so everyone could go home at the end of the day.

"In a way, that was the scary part for me, being around Lionel and his ominous presence," Anderson confesses. "It made you say to yourself, 'Am I any good to be here with him?'"

Hollywood columnist Louella Parsons noted of Barrymore's performance as Mr. Potter: "In all his years of acting, he has never been as powerful a heavy. But he can play either the kindest person or the meanest, with equal facility. That's because he knows both the heart and technique of acting." Below: Hollywood's "mad hatter," gossip columnist Hedda Hopper, was one of Lionel Barrymore's biggest fans and wrote glowingly of his portrayal as old man Potter.

About the "Little Fella"

Frank Capra pegged it. He knew that Clarence Odbody AS2 could only be portrayed by Henry Travers, a little man of Irish descent, and a gentleman through and through. With that sweet doughy face and whiskery eyebrows, Travers looked like a leprechaun and his squeaky voice matched the charm.

Born Travers John Geagerty on March 5, 1874 at Berwick-on-Tweed, Northumberland, England, he ambitiously began a career on stage at the age of eighteen and emigrated to America in 1901; in New York he landed some stage roles and became a charter member of the Theatre Guild one year later. Changing his name, he appeared in more than twenty plays on Broadway until he eventually found his way to Hollywood in the early 1930s, where he embarked on a film career and appeared in more than fifty films in the next several decades. The role of Clarence the angel was one of his last. Henry was married twice and got his wings on October 18, 1965, when he was ninety-one years old.

Henry Travers, the enchanting little actor with a marshmallow face, retired from motion pictures not long after his role as Clarence.

Known for playing granddads and gray-hairs most of his career, Travers was perfect to star on Broadway in the celebrated role of Grandpa Sycamore in George Kaufman and Moss Hart's smash hit play *You Can't Take It With You* in 1936. (Ironically, in Frank Capra's 1938 film version of *You Can't Take It With You,* the role was played by Lionel Barrymore.)

Travers was nominated for an Academy Award for Best Supporting Actor as Mr. Ballard, the station-master in the film *Mrs. Miniver* (1942). Some of his best film appearances include: *The Invisible Man* (1933), *Death Takes a Holiday* (1934), *Pursuit* (1935), *The Sisters* (1938), *Dark Victory* (1939), *Edison, the Man* (1940), *High Sierra* (1941), and *The Bells of St. Mary's* (1945).

Peggy Hess was just fourteen when her grandfather died, but she remembers her famous grandfather well:

My grandfather spoke very little of his movies, but he did seem to like *Mrs. Miniver* the best. I'm not sure why he retired, but he wasn't working when I was little and used to visit. I remember him walking with the help of a cane, so perhaps it was that he was just getting too old. Grandpa was exactly like he was in his movies, always even-tempered. I never heard him raise his voice at anyone. He was the type of person who thought about what he would say before he said it, so when he said something, people listened.

My grandmother was his second wife and she had three children by her first husband. My father was the youngest. Grandpa never had any biological children, but always loved his step kids. We had lots of fun at Easter, I remember that well. We'd visit from Northern California and we'd always take family photos.

My grandfather liked to sit in a big chair in his office, read, and drink whisky on the rocks. He and my father got along well because they liked the same things (only my father liked to drink wine in those days). They would spend their time outside under the palm trees in the garden when the weather was nice and sometimes they would tell us kids stories.

My grandparents lived in Hollywood in a nice home off Sunset on a street called Stanley Boulevard. It was three doors up on the west side, from the preview house on the corner of Sunset. Back in those days, it was a very nice neighborhood. They lived in a California-style home, light color stucco; it was not pink but sort of between pink and pale yellow, hard to describe, but very nice. It had a tile roof, boxwood hedges and a nice back yard with date palm trees. They added on to the back of the house and had a guest suite where my sisters and I usually stayed. There was a beautiful sunroom in the house where my grandparents had coffee in every morning.

Naturally, *It's a Wonderful Life* is a family tradition for us on Christmas Eve. My grandfather was not a religious person that I recall. We celebrated (Catholic) holidays but that is because my mother is Catholic. Gary Cooper was a family friend and had converted to Catholicism. My grandparents had talked to the Coopers and Gary Cooper gave me a book of the Saints for my confirmation, so I guess they had discussed it.

Grandpa's voice was exactly as you hear it in the movies. It was funny because when I was a teen, his movies would come on television and if I wasn't watching I would still recognize his voice. I remember *High Sierra* came on and I was listening but not paying a lot of attention until my Grandfather's voice came on. I didn't even know he had worked with Humphrey Bogart. That gentle friendly squeaky-voiced person you see on film is exactly who Henry Travers was. He was very unpretentious. He was casual, friendly, and a real angel.

Henry Travers played Bette Davis's father in a rather forgettable film, The Sisters *(1938).*

Jimmy Stewart's Wonderful Life

Amid full swing of the *It's a Wonderful Life* revival in America, actor Jimmy Stewart shared his thoughts about the film in an article for the *Los Angeles Herald-Examiner,* which appeared in print Christmas day, 1984, as a present for readers. Interviewed by editor Mitchell Fink, the seventy-six-year-old actor reiterated that of his eighty-plus films, this was indeed his most cherished.

Strange as it seems to us, It's a Wonderful Life *was not a hit when it came out, was it?*

No. It did fair business, but it wasn't a hit. It was the first picture done by a new company formed right after the war by Frank Capra, William Wyler, George Stevens, and Sam Briskin, the company being Liberty Films. This picture was the first for Liberty.

Wasn't It's a Wonderful Life *your first picture after the war?*

Yes, that's correct.

Did either you or Frank have the feeling that It's a Wonderful Life *would leave the kind of lasting impression that it obviously has?*

Well, we were both excited about the picture and everything. It was sort of a tryout thing for both of us. We had been away, I had been away for four and a half years. This got me back into the acting business. Frank had been away, he had made a lot of training films. So there was a lot of uncertainty for both of us. The thing that makes me so loyal and so admire the film was that it came at that particular time, and that as we got into it more and more, we both completely fell in love with the thing and everybody else did. Everybody was so excited about it and liked the idea of the picture so much. I must say that it was a tremendous thing for me.

First to have Capra, second to have this type of story as my first picture back.

How did Capra go about explaining the projects to you?

I had this house in Brentwood. I rented it when I went into the service. When I got back, the folks there had been there for so long that they wouldn't let me in! So I stayed up with Hank Fonda. We'd fly kites and we played with his kids and so on. Frank called me on the phone at Hank's. He said, "Come over. I've got sort of an idea for a picture."

So I went over and he started telling me about this fellow in this small town and he's gonna kill himself and Frank says, "There's an angel named Clarence on the bridge where this fellow's gonna drown himself. Clarence comes down and Clarence can't swim, so the fellow has to save Clarence. The angel wants to win his wings, but he's supposed to take care of this guy. When you say you wish you'd never been born, the angel sort of looks up, gets the OK, so you've never been born. All right?"

All right? I didn't know what the hell Frank was talking about—angel? Clarence? But he went on, and he went on, and it just grew on me. I must say that the crowd he got together—Lionel Barrymore and Tom Mitchell and Donna Reed and Frank Faylen

Above: *Potter lights up George.* Below: *Briefly seduced by Potter's spell, George abruptly spouts his "scurvy little spider" speech aimed in the eye of Potter—and his goon, too!*

George licks his lips with wild abandon, but his plan for a frisky night out with Violet embarrassingly grabs everybody's attention.

and Henry Travers, so many of them I'll never forget.

You feel a great attachment to the film, don't you?

Yes, and you know it was different from most other pictures then in that it wasn't from a play, it wasn't from a book, it wasn't from an actual happening. Frank got it as a sort of footnote, or a P.S. to a letter. Little phrases like "No one's born to be a failure."

You mean, he could create an entire story line from a phrase like that?

Well, the phrase meant something. Or, "A man's never poor if he has friends." I mean, that's all. When you think about it, so much of the picture is based on those two phrases. But Frank took those two things, gave it to Hackett and Goodrich and they just ate it up. They worked the story out with Frank.

All of Capra's films seem to have that thread, that of the common man rising up against the forces of evil. When you got the script to It's a

Colonel James Stewart arrives home from the war an honest to goodness hero, greeted by his proud parents, Mr. and Mrs. Alexander Stewart, at the St. Regis Hotel in New York City. (September 1945)

Just a few years after Wonderful Life, Jimmy Stewart became an old family man himself. Shown in this 1951 Stewart family portrait are Jimmy with his wife, Gloria, her two sons from a former marriage, Michael and Ronald, and the new additions, twins Judy and Kelly.

75

Wonderful Life, *what did you think about your character, George Bailey?*

Everything happened so fast after Frank got the idea and the script, getting the cast together and getting things started, that I didn't have much time to think about what I was going to do with the George Bailey character.

Before I knew what was happening, I was in it. This worked me a little. Four and a half years not doing anything, and coming back to a demanding thing worked me. I'll always be grateful to Lionel Barrymore. He sensed this. He gave me such wonderful encouragement in the beginning.

Being away for four and a half years, did you think you had lost it, your ability to act?

That's why Lionel Barrymore was so important to me. He told me not to apologize for not being in town the last four years. He told me to just do it, not to make excuses, or feel sorry for myself. It was wonderful for me. I'll always be grateful.

When we watch it, it seems to be the same Jimmy Stewart, so natural. There were fears though?

At first, yes.

How long did the film take to shoot?

Six, seven weeks. At the old Columbia lot. And much of it was done at night. Long nights. One of the many problems had to do with the shooting all night. I don't remember it ever happening before or since. It'd get to be 5 o'clock and the birds would start singing. How are you going to get the birds to stop singing? Not even

Capra could do that. But he worked it out. . . . A stuntman had a pet crow who did as it was told. When the birds starting chirping, he'd say "Get them!" and the crow would scare the birds away. True story.

Was the film shot in sequence?

Yes, we very seldom went out of sequence.

Because of the story line, did shooting in sequence cause everyone to get caught up in what was happening?

Yes. I remember when Frank decided this. It never went out of sequence unless it was something that didn't matter much. It kept the story building and building and building.

Do you think that's a problem with a lot of movies today? That they aren't shot in sequence?

That has always been a problem with the movies. If you are in the picture business, this is one of the things you have to learn. People say, "I liked the movie because everybody was so natural." Well, making a movie is probably one of the most unnatural things there is. But sometimes it works. I think working out of context is something we used to try not to do. Working in context with *It's a Wonderful Life* sort of linked everybody to the story. I can't think of anybody better than Frank Capra when it came to handling a cast, where everybody is caught up with the idea of the story, which continued all through the shooting of the movie.

It was rare to see Jimmy Stewart without his toupée, especially later in life. This photo, taken at the Pentagon in March 1960, shows Stewart, who held the rank of brigadier general in the Air Force Reserve, when he served some active duty in Washington. With Stewart is Brig. Gen. Eugene LeBailey.

This may seem like a ridiculous question, but why don't they make films like that anymore?

I think the timing of the film was of tremendous importance. Right after the war.

But some people say the film wasn't a big hit because it came out right after the war, and maybe it was a little too soft a story for that time.

Could be. It's hard to put your finger on a thing like that. It was nominated for all kinds of awards. *Best Years of Our Lives* won just about everything that year. I've never talked to anybody, including Frank, about why. Maybe it did come out at the wrong time. I just had the feeling as we progressed that it had something all its own and originality like no other picture I've been in.

How many films have you made?

Eighty-one, give or take.

Is It's a Wonderful Life *your favorite?*

Yes.

It's probably a lot of people's favorite. People look forward to it every Christmas. It seems to fill some void. Why?

It's the time of year when we think about family, the importance of faith in God, the importance of community spirit.

George Bailey was a small-town, decent guy. Today, guys like George Bailey are probably having it rougher than George Bailey did.

You're right. He does have a much rougher time today, but I think the way George Bailey is presented is a very good example of the hard-working fellow with the family having a tough time of it against the big shots. It points the idea up clearer than a lot of other pictures.

Do you still watch it during the holidays?

Yeah, I have a copy of it.

Do you watch a lot of your old films?

I see some of them, if they don't come on too late. If they're on late, I fall asleep.

How do you feel when you're watching yourself as a much younger man?

I found out a lot about that with the reissuing of the Hitchcock pictures. They are twenty, thirty years old. I can remember seeing them in sneak previews, which were frightening to me. I felt that as an actor, I had to go and look at the thing, have an opinion on it, but I didn't help myself much because whether you admit it or not, you end up just looking at yourself. I keep saying, "Why didn't they use the other take?" I end up at the end of the picture completely frustrated, not knowing whether the picture was good because I was just looking at myself.

My mother used to say, when the picture would play back in Indiana, Pennsylvania, it'd usually play three days. She'd go to every performance, but not until the last two performances would she write to me about it because she was always just looking at me, and she didn't know what the hell the story was about, or anything.

My father would only go Saturday night after the store closed. He would call me up every once in a while to talk about it, and I could tell exactly when he'd fell asleep. He'd start wandering about the plot, and I'd check with my mother, and she'd say, "Yes, that's about right."

Does it take you repeated viewings to get away from you and start looking at the film?

Yes. In the Hitchcock pictures, when we first started drumming them up, they had a film festival in New York. I met the press. They showed *Rear Window,* which I hadn't seen in twenty years, and I sat back and loved it. It was fine. I saw that young fellow with all that hair, and he seemed to be getting laughs and everything and I enjoyed it. And what a beautiful thing Grace Kelly was.

I did the same thing with *The Glenn Miller Story.* There again, I hadn't seen it for twenty years.

It's incredible to think, as we speak, It's a Wonderful Life is playing in a local theater, and will be all over the TV screen during the holidays. That sets this film apart, doesn't it?

Sure. The ending is Christmas Eve, that's a part of it. I'm holding my daughter, and one of the bells rings on the Christmas tree and she says, "Every time a bell rings, an angel gets his wings." I look up and say, "Good luck, Clarence." This is an amazing story, so a part of the Christmas idea. People have asked me if it's a success story, but it doesn't quite fit that. It's more than that. No man is born to be a failure. Frank was right.

Oddly enough, there are people who have never seen It's a Wonderful Life. Let's say they all promise to watch it on Christmas. What message, if any, do you want to bring to them?

That nobody is born to be a failure, and no man is poor if he has friends. You just enlarge on those two things, and there's not much more to say.

(REPRINTED BY PERMISSION OF THE UNIVERSITY OF SOUTHERN CALIFORNIA LIBRARY / HEARST NEWSPAPER COLLECTIONS; COURTESY OF ACADEMY OF MOTION PICTURE ARTS & SCIENCES)

3

꘡ ꘡ ꘡ ꘡

And All the Trimmings

One of the most aggravating, hair-pulling tasks associated with producing this story, according to Frank Capra, was cutting the precious scenes he'd painstakingly put on film. Capra worked with some exceptionally talented cinematographers to capture the scenes: Joseph Walker, Joseph Biroc, and Victor Milner. Walker, who collaborated closely with Capra on many of the director's features films dating back to the silents, was forced to leave *It's a Wonderful Life* after a few weeks in order to fulfill a previous commitment at Columbia Pictures. Capra promoted Joseph Biroc from camera operator to lead cameraman.

"I remember I was sitting on the crane and Capra came up to me," Biroc told Jimmy Hawkins in *The It's a Wonderful Life Trivia Book*. "He was grinning from ear to ear and came right out and asked me, 'How would you like to take over the picture?' . . . That was it. From that moment on I was the cameraman. First thing I shot was the night stuff, in the cemetery, all that snow on the ground. Worst thing in the world to work with. The snow's so bright you can't light it the way it should look with some shadows."

RKO's press campaign book for the film notes, "From an exposed 350,000 feet of film, Capra and his film editor, William Hornbeck, began work in cutting it to approximately 11,900 feet." The rest, as they say, ended up on the editor's cutting room floor. It had to be a tedious thing, maybe even maddening, to trim these scenes and throw them away for good. Granted, not all of that discarded footage contains additional scenes. There are bad takes, retakes, and mistakes on film that had to be junked. Still, wouldn't it be fascinating to see the "lost" footage anyway?

Capra's eye for just the right angle and "take" on film was impeccable and he worked closely with Hornbeck to choose these shots from the unending reels of footage. It was Capra's style of directing that created such a voluminous amount of footage. He told the *New Orleans Review* in 1981: "Yes, actors are supposed to commit their lines to memory. I deliberately discouraged it. It's heresy, but I want the human person to emerge out of a believable situation and not to be preset. I used a lot of first takes for that reason; about 75 percent of my scenes were first takes. They weren't polished, they had slight hesitation, they were imperfect. But they had freshness and were believable. And the audience liked those scenes."

✠ ✠ ✠

What has recently been discovered are rare unpublished photographs depicting scenes Capra had crystallized onto celluloid. Long buried in several archives, these photographs accompany excerpts from early scripts of *It's a Wonderful Life* which can provide for you a glimpse into the "lost" moments. Whether these precious scenes stricken from the final

This rare candid photograph shows Stewart and Reed practicing the Charleston during a rehearsal.

RICHARD GOODSON COLLECTION

film would have helped or hindered is your call, but it's seductive to contemplate these interludes and how they may have played out and affected the rest of the story.

The biggest question is: Why did Capra choose to snip the amazing scene of Clarence's stern face-to-face admonishment of Potter at the end of the film? He must have pondered it countless times. Must the villain be reformed? It's a matter of taste, not formula. With that bit of business unresolved, it guarantees much for the viewer's imagination. Capra must have felt it best; besides, real life tells us that not all reprobates pay for their dirty deeds, so in this story Capra left it as an open wound—not to be healed until *Saturday Night Live*'s parody brought brutal justice to Potter decades later.

╬╬╬╬╬╬

Utilizing much of Frank Capra's archives held at Wesleyan University, film historian Jeanine Basinger described in *The It's a Wonderful Life Book* the evolution of scripts and scribes for this film: "More than a year before Frank Capra purchased 'The Greatest Gift' from RKO, three complete versions of the script had already been written. These three scripts—all unsatisfactory—have for many years been presumed lost or destroyed. Capra had bought them as part of his original deal but had discarded them for a complete rewrite by Frances Goodrich and Albert Hackett. He frequently referred to the three scripts in interviews, crediting them to Marc Connelly, Dalton

This rare photograph shows much more of Sam Wainwright's New York office set than the film, including a portrait nearby of sweet Mary Hatch. Was Sam Wainwright a two-timer?

USC CINEMA-TELEVISION LIBRARY

Strange, But True

You'll see a lot of strange things from now on.
⌁ CLARENCE

Once again, George's hopes for getting out of town are shot when he realizes he must stay on with the Building and Loan. The black bird perched on Uncle Billy's arm, known as Jimmie the Raven, appeared in several of Capra's films, as well as in the MGM classic The Wizard of Oz. (Left to right: Jimmie the Raven, Thomas Mitchell, Charles Williams, Harry Cheshire, Mary Treen, and Jimmy Stewart).

Mr. Carter, the bank examiner (Charles Halton), hurries the situation because he wants to spend Christmas in Elmira with his family.

Yes, there are a few myths, misconceptions, and misnomers that have sprouted from the half-century legacy of *It's a Wonderful Life.* Some of them have spun way out of control, perpetuated into everyday trivia. Here's the scoop to help untwist some of those tales into straight fact for you.

- **Not Granted** It's been said many times that Frank Capra originally intended Cary Grant to play George Bailey. Originally, when the story "The

Greatest Gift" had been purchased by RKO Radio Pictures, it was to be a vehicle for Grant, but that version didn't get produced. Eventually, when the screen property landed in the hands of Capra, it became *It's a Wonderful Life* and the director had only two actors in mind for the prized role: Henry Fonda and James Stewart.

- **Oh Christmas Tree!** Naturally, every family has their sacred holiday traditions, especially when it comes to trim-

Yep, that's Carl Switzer (Alfalfa from the Our Gang comedies) who devilishly opens the gym floor after George irks him. Many who knew Switzer would agree that this role wasn't far off from his actual, mischievous personality.

ming the tree. Odd though, for a movie about angels—with a memorable Christmas Eve scene to outshine all others—notice how the Bailey family puts atop their tree a glistening star rather than an angel. Not that there's anything wrong with that . . .

- **Never Mind!** A short documentary produced in 1990 about the making of *It's a Wonderful Life* (hosted by Tom Bosley) proclaimed one memorable scene in the film to be an "accident" on the part of actor Thomas Mitchell. Following the wedding reception at the Bailey home, there is a brief porch scene where Uncle Billy drunkenly stumbles away (off camera, with an audible crash). He yells out, "I'm all right, I'm allllll right!" Sorry to disappoint any trivia buffs, but that little sequence was no blunder. It occurs in the film exactly as it was planned and written in the final script, even according to the earlier written treatments.

- **Talk About Wings** It's true Frank Capra had a great connection with nature, but what is it with the bird references in this film? We see Jimmy the Raven perched prominently in the Building & Loan office. (Owned and trained by Curly Twifard for more than thirty years, it was the same raven that appeared in *The Wizard of Oz* as a crow on the Scarecrow's shoulder.) Jimmy was a favorite of Capra's and the director used the obedient feathered friend in other films. But have you snared the rest of the references nestled in the film's dialogue? Mr. Gower warns young

George in the drugstore: "You're not paid to be a canary." Mr. Potter is called a buzzard. The high school principal is named Mr. Partridge. George admits to his father that he couldn't stand to be "cooped up" in a shabby little office. What about Mary Hatch? During the downpour, the man hanging signs wonders if George and Mary are a pair of ducks. Inside, Mary is cooking chickens on a spit in the fireplace. And then there is the scene where George lassos the stork and asks his wife if she's "on the nest?" Hmmmmmmmmmm.

- **Word on the Street . . .** It would be nice to believe the legend that the late Jim Henson named his two famous *Sesame Street* muppet pals, Ernie and Bert, after the film's secondary characters Ernie the cabdriver and Bert the cop. But it's just not so, say people in their neighborhood. It's purely a coincidence, admit Henson representatives who were there in the late 1960s when *Sesame Street* first paved its way on television.

- **Whoops!** Watch for the daytime scene when proud George Bailey walks around snow-covered Bedford Falls passing out newspapers with his brother Harry on the front cover shown being honored by the president. He's toting a Christmas wreath slung on his arm. In the next shot, George enters the Building & Loan and tosses the wreath onto a desk and then takes the phone call. But wait, in the next shot, the wreath is mysteriously still hanging on his arm.

Trumbo, and Clifford Odets, but indicated he did not recollect saving them."

Actually, they do survive, as well as an additional uncredited script and two more working scripts held in the archive of the Academy of Motion Pictures Arts and Sciences. Together, all of them provide a picture of the well that Capra drew from, utilizing varied elements and influences from each of the drafts: Marc Connelly (who contributed the first rough draft in August 1944), introduced a heaven at the beginning of the story with characters "discussing man's fate." Connelly's versions take many twists and turns while being revised and eventually shelved. The Clifford Odets treatments include familiar storylines that ended up in the final film: Young Harry nearly drowning on the ice; George and Mary in a moonlit dance, interrupted by the news of the death of George's father; and Little Zuzu in this script had a much larger role. However, in Odets's story there is no Mr. Potter, and the writer incorporates two distinct Georges—one good, one bad—and they duke it out on the bridge.

The earlier versions all lack "depth, humor, and friendship," according to Basinger. Capra, along with Goodrich and Hackett, changed all that and created more believable characters with warmth. In this new treatment, Capra leads the viewer through all emotions in life's spectrum—joy, sadness, despair, guilt, pity, apathy, and all the splendor in God's greatest gift of human life. His film journey is much like life itself and it takes us through happiness to anger, from honesty to deceit, and shows life and death, all rolled into *It's a Wonderful Life*. Although his contribution to the scripts is rarely documented fully, Capra indeed helped mold the characters with lines and details all of his own doing. He was a supremely detail-oriented producer and director, right down to movement and sound, and most of the actors who worked with him expressed appreciation for such dedication.

Surviving in the Capra Archives are an estimating script for *It's a Wonderful Life* (dated March 20, 1946) used to calculate costs and plan the budget, and a final script as shot (dated March 4, 1947), which is basically a transcript of the final film presentation as we know it. The Motion Picture Academy's library has preserved

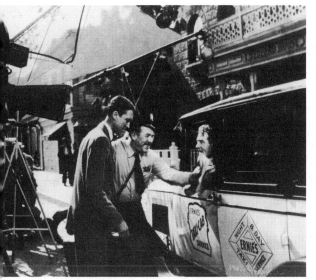

another script dated March 18, 1946. Gear up your imagination as you discover some of the remarkable (sometimes minor) scenes in this script that were obviously removed, but more importantly, these scenes were thought to have been stricken prior to production and never filmed. These rare unpublished photographs attest otherwise and provide a fascinating look at what might have been in Bedford Falls.

Filming a scene that was eventually trimmed are George, Bert the cop, and Ernie the cabbie. Uncle Billy's black bird, actually named Jimmie the Raven, lands on George's arm as they drive away.

꧁꧂꧁꧂꧁꧂

Capra's early version of the film's opening is like day and night, quite literally. The movie opens with the sight of a bright heaven, the credits and titles superimposed over "beautiful moving clouds . . . giving the impression of rising up from the earth." This camera movement was to be accompanied by the music of Beethoven's Ninth.

Rather than just voices heard from the celestial image, like we're used to experiencing in the beginning, Capra wanted to open with heaven—precisely in the interior of Ben Franklin's office and work-shop. Ben Franklin is now an angel, but still working on inventions in heaven. Joseph, another angel, pops in to see Franklin and explains about a tired, disillusioned man on earth who needs their help. Franklin fidgets with some experimental machinery in his "lab" and turns some loudspeakers and dials and knobs until he is able to hear the prayers coming from Bedford Falls, New York. They get the help of a young black call boy (dressed like the famous Phillip Morris cigarette page boy named "Johnny," which was popular at the time) to summon Clarence, the wild-eyed childlike angel-wannabe.

During the conversation, a very interesting exchange between Joseph and Clarence has been cut. In Clarence's voice, he explains how he went to work in his wife's father's clock shop and how he hated it but grew to conquer it. "You see, I put my musical soul right into those confounded clocks. . . . Today all over the world, my chimes are ringing . . . ding dong, ding dong!"

The rest of the film's opening sequence follows the final script, with Clarence becoming familiar with George's life from the beginning. This script also includes a longer ice pond scene in which young George pelts a snowball at young Mary and hits her in the face.

†◊†◊†◊†

Dated May 7, 1946, by Capra in the script: In his notes, Capra handwrote the concept for this scene in which Uncle Billy's black bird, Jimmy, lands on Mr. Potter's hand and pecks him, causing the ol' codger to make a trip to the drugstore for some antiseptic to clean the wound. His hand is wrapped in cloth as he enters Gower's drugstore near the end of the sequence. This scene was actually shot, but cut from the film.

This deleted bit follows directly after George has picked up his new second-hand suitcase and heads over to his old stomping grounds to thank Mr. Gower for the customized luggage. This time, the drugstore is loaded with kids drinking ice cream sodas. It's the place to be in Bedford Falls. As the script describes: "Gower is a different man now—sober, shaven, and good humored. He is behind the counter waiting on customers when George comes in. Gower's face lights up when he sees George." Immediately, George triggers the bulky vintage cigar lighter and wishes for a million dollars. Hot dog!

GEORGE

Gee whiz—my old soda fountain! Well, ye olde apothecary shoppe ain't what she used to be, is it?

GOWER

After school they swarm in here like ants. Come over here.
>(starts putting cigarettes in George's pocket)

So you're leaving? Always knew those *National Geographics* would get you.

GEORGE

Gee . . . thanks, Mr. Gower.

GOWER

How long will you be gone?

GEORGE

Three months. Coming back for college in the fall.

GOWER

>(surprised)

College? Thought you gave up that idea when you went in with your father in the Building and Loan?

GEORGE

Nope, nope, nope. Been working there the last three years to get enough money to see me through school, that's all—Lookit here . . .
>(pulls out bank book and shows it to Gower)

You're the one that started me . . . with that big buck a week you used to pay me.

GOWER

>(reading the bank book)

Fourteen hundred! George you can get married and have kids with that.

GEORGE

>(taking back the book)

Nooope, nope, nope, nope.

GOWER

George, I'll sell you half interest in my place for that!

GEORGE

Noooope, nope, nope, nope.
>(Some of the kids nearby take it up.)

KIDS

Noooope, nope, nope, nope.

The images on these pages provide a rare glimpse into a scene that was filmed but ultimately cut. A fresh George Bailey jokes around with the kids in Gower's Drug Store and then comes face to face with Mr. Potter in the doorway on his way out.

GEORGE
(good humouredly, turning to kids)

Noooope, nope, nope, nope.

GOWER

George, you aren't thinking of leaving Bedford Falls for good?

GEORGE

Nooope, nope . . . Yeeooop, yep, yep, yep.

GOWER
(getting the spirit)

Nope, nope, nope, nope.

Potter comes in the door and watches proceedings with a vinegar face.

GEORGE
(to Gower)

Goodbyeeee, goodbye, goodbye, goodbye.
(shakes his hand)

KIDS

Goodbyeeeee, goodbye, goodbye. Nooope, nope, nope. Yeeoop, yep, yep.

Everybody starts shouting their own version. George waves at them and starts hur-

riedly out. He runs into Potter, grabbing his hand, George pumps it up and down.

GEORGE
(to Potter)
Goodbyeeeeee, Goodbye, goodbye, goodbye.

POTTER
(disgusted)
No wonder the country's going to pot.

GEORGE
(with a knowing look toward kids)
Well, as long as it doesn't go to Potter! Ha, ha!

A shriek of laughter from the kids, as George runs out. Gower laughs explosively, but laugh freezes on his face as he catches Potter's vinegar look.

❧❧❧

Capra had added little bit more action for Annie the maid in the scene following the lively wedding reception at the Bailey home. Drunken Uncle Billy has already grabbed his hat and stumbled toward home. Ma Bailey has had a quiet talk with George and convinced him to go visit Mary Hatch at home.

GEORGE
Mother o' mine, I see right through you to your back collar button—want to get rid of me, don't you?

MOTHER
(fondly gives him his hat)
Yes. George, here's your hat—what's your hurry?

GEORGE
I'll beat you over the head with a baseball bat.
(kisses her—looks up and sees Harry and wife inside)

He goes to the edge of the porch, looks up at the star-studded sky. Annie listens in from the doorway.

GEORGE
(cont'd)

A lot of stars out tonight . . . did you know that the nearest star is over twenty-five trillion miles away from the earth?

CLOSEUP—Mother. Her face suddenly sad and wistful as she looks toward George.

GEORGE'S VOICE

Gosh, that'd be some trip, wouldn't it?

MED SHOT.

ANNIE
(moves into scene)

If you're going that far, better take your hat.
(holds out his hat)

GEORGE

Sure, Annie, old pal, old pal.
(imitating Uncle Billy)

Which one's mine?

ANNIE

The end one.

George grabs an imaginary end hat, puts his on his head.

In this scene cut from the film, Annie comes out and gives George his hat before he heads off to see Mary.

†‡†‡†‡†‡

Cut from the film was a brief, intimate scene between Violet and George in his office at the Building and Loan. The Bank Examiner has arrived and Violet is waiting for George at his office as well. When George arrives, he escorts her into his private office and shuts the door. Violet explains that she is leaving for New York City and George sits at his desk and begins to type a letter of recommendation on official Building and Loan Association stationery. He types, and speaks simultaneously: "Miss Violet Bick has been employed as a clerk by this company for the past two years . . ."

"That's a lie, George," she interrupts.

He continues typing. George grabs the letter, signs it, folds it, and gives it to her before reaching into his pocket and then handing her some cash to take with her. Violet then kisses him in gratitude.

According to earlier scripts, in his office George gave more to Violet than just a few bucks.

+:+ +:+ +:+

This highly emotional moment between Mary and George was cut from the film, and it's anyone's guess why. It occurs after George has spend the day searching for the lost eight thousand dollars and returns home a nervous wreck, angry, and appearing like he's aged ten years overnight. He has yelled at the children, shoved furniture around, and stormed out of the house in desperation with his insurance policy in hand. George exits through the front door, rather than get on the telephone (as the film depicts). Mary follows George outside. George hesitates and leans up against a railing on the porch, deeply hurt and miserable at the suffering he's caused. Mary comes out the front door and quietly takes his arm. She knows something is terribly wrong.

MARY

I'm sorry dear.

GEORGE

Mary Hatch—please believe me—Mary Hatch, I love you very, very much.
He kisses her and walks away, all the while contemplating some way out of his mess, or worse yet—suicide.

+:+ +:+ +:+

This brief, humorous exchange was cut from the film. Directly after drunken George slams his automobile into a tree in the snowstorm, the indignant owner of the house comes out and complains.

It's anyone's guess why this brief poignant scene was clipped from the film. When despondent George leaves the house contemplating suicide, Mary runs after him. Before running off, George takes one last look at his wife and quietly assures her that he loves her.

OWNER

My great-grandfather planted that tree!

GEORGE

Is your great-grandfather still alive?

OWNER

No!

GEORGE

Then what does he care?

༝༝༝

In an earlier script, Clarence escorts a bewildered George around Pottersville, where they discover some bizarre sights and occurrences, including the fate of his Italian friend, Mr. Martini. Clarence leads him to the cemetery and shows him something very startling—the Martini family tombstone. He tells George, "Since there was no Bailey Park, the Martinis never moved out of Potter's slums. Fire burnt down several houses one year."

༝༝༝

It's obvious why Frank Capra struck this unusual scene. This kooky bit gave more for actor Frank Faylen to do on-camera, including some physical pratfalls, but the action just didn't fit the situation and it hardly furthered the story in any constructive way.

George insists on finding Mary Hatch, now a spinster working at the library. In a daze, he follows her and grabs her, quizzing "Mary, it's me, George! Don't you know me? What's happened to us?" Mary breaks away from George's grasp and runs away screaming, eventually heading into a small café and beer parlor. In the interior of the beer parlor, there are small tables, booths, a counter. The script calls for the place to be crowded: "Many of the people are the same who were present during the run on the Building and Loan."

The camera cuts to Ernie the cab driver who is drinking and explaining about seeing a "ghost" at the old house on Sycamore Street to "a Negro friend in a janitor uniform," as the script describes. Mary comes running in, screaming. The place is in an uproar when George enters, practically insane.

The camera goes in for a shot of Ernie and the janitor in the beer parlor's front booth. A closeup catches Ernie's eyes pop out of his head as he sees George. "That's him!" he yells, and then he turns and crashes right through the front window, followed by the janitor.

Restrained by some of the patrons, a crazed George he calls for Clarence's help. The camera then goes for a closeup of Clarence peering in through the large hole in the window. On hearing George call his name, his face lights up like he's expecting this to happen. George starts to dash away and Bert the cop follows outside, gets in a fracas with George, then pulls out his gun and begins to fire at George in the distance.

The crowd comes rushing out of the café and Bert has gone after George. The camera goes in for a closeup of Ernie, now in the doorway inadvertently talking to Clarence, who is standing there eating an apple.

In a scene cut from the film, Clarence causes a catastrophe in the busy pub.

USC CINEMA-TELEVISION LIBRARY

> ERNIE
> (excitedly)
> He's a ghost, I tell you. And the other one was a little old guy, just about your—
> (he freezes stiff as he recognizes Clarence)
> Yoweee!
> *Ernie turns and runs smack into a brick wall, as the camera dissolves out.*

꘠ ꘠ ꘠

Frank Capra must have deliberated on this decision for a while. In a climax that would've capped the final moments of the movie just perfectly, Clarence cleverly puts Potter in his place. So why peel away this fulfilling scene from the film? Maybe Capra felt it drove the "richest man in town" theme a little too far. This is the comeuppance that Frank Capra had originally intended. Oh, to see this lost footage.

After George's "rebirth" at the bridge, he runs through Bedford Falls hollering Merry Christmas—even to ol' man Potter. (How forgiving.)

POTTER

And a happy New Year in jail. Go on home—they're waiting for
you.

(to goon)

Well, I can go home now—go get the carriage.

As the goon exits, Potter suddenly sees Clarence seated in a chair, calmly munch-
ing an apple.

POTTER

(cont'd)

Who are you? How'd you get in here? What are you doing?

CLARENCE

Don't really know, myself. You're none of my business, you know.
Joseph won't like it, either.

Potter reaches for telephone.

CLARENCE

(cont'd)

Uh, uh. I wouldn't call the police. Besides, if they come I'd have to
tell them of the money you stole from Uncle Billy.

Potter's hand leaves phone.

CLARENCE

(cont'd)

That was a wicked thing to do. It not only made you a thief; it
almost made you a murderer. You almost killed George Bailey
tonight.

(looking up)

Coming. I'm not going to Coney Island.

Coming! Are you going to let this old stinkpot get away with this?

(to Potter)

You're an old man, Henry Potter; bitter, selfish and lonely. You're
going to die soon—then what? Can you think of anyone in the
world—man, woman, child or animal, that would care? Think
hard, Potter, are you the richest man around here, or the poorest?

Clarence disappears, leaving just the core of his apple.

The Prayer Scene

Jimmy Stewart stated that this scene from *It's a Wonderful Life*, the unforgettable sequence where George Bailey sits at a bar, lonely and defeated, was his favorite in the film. There's not a more gripping moment than when George thinks seriously of throwing away God's greatest gift but desperately prays for help first. (Interestingly, in a 1987 TV special/documentary about his life hosted by Johnny Carson, the actor *also* described the scene where he and Clarence warm up in the little bridge tollhouse as his favorite.)

During this gripping sequence, George quietly prays to God for direction while a Corsican song, "Vieni, Vieni," haunts the background. Capra knew the music would help weave an eerie texture to the tavern scene as the camera crept in to penetrate such an intimate moment of desperation.

Even a staunch agnostic must admit: the energy and intensity in this "prayer scene" is electrifying.

Entertainer Carol Burnett, a longtime unabashed fan of Jimmy Stewart, did not mince her words of admiration for her favorite actor and this powerfully pivotal scene. "I think it's one of the finest pieces of work that anyone has ever done on the screen," she said. "That moment, at that bar, it's indelible in my mind. He realizes that he has lost everything. The money is missing. It's Christmas Eve. And he sits there and starts to cry. He is so in tune with that character and that writing that he and George Bailey are one."

Capra felt the setting was key in making this scene effective. To increase the intimacy, the director zoomed into George tightly. This was one of those "tricky scenes" in the film that could very well backfire if it wasn't handled delicately to properly illustrate a mood swing. "Well, he says a prayer . . . 'Oh God, I'm at the end of my rope. Show me the way.' It's a short prayer but we believe it. He's desperate and has nowhere to turn," said Capra in 1981. "If we showed him on his knees in church or in a private corner, the audience wouldn't take to it. But in a bar, right after gulping down a shot of whiskey, we are inclined to believe it. Then, a man recognizes him as the one who told off his schoolteacher wife on the phone and socks him. That's what he gets for praying. That's natural. Someone expects immediate help and look what happens. A man is blue so he drinks—but it opens him up. You see inside the man. That deepens the story and helps the interest."

On the Air

Remember radio? In the grandest era of the medium, radio was not just for music and news, it was one of our main forms of entertainment. From the 1920s to the 1950s, the radio served as a vital part of our communications explosion in America. Millions of listeners had their favorite drama series or comedy shows that they comfortably sat and listened to in the living room or while eating dinner with the family. It was a ritual for many families to gather around the radio and actually concentrate on the audio entertainment coming from a nicely designed wooden box that was stationed prominently in the house's main room.

It was not uncommon in the 1940s to recreate a movie story on radio, even just on the heels of the film's big-screen release. With *It's a Wonderful Life,* the story of George Bailey's fall into despair and rescue by an angel was first adapted for radio on CBS radio's *Lux Radio Theatre* show.

Originally broadcast on March 10, 1947, just a few months after the film's release, the one-hour truncated *Lux Radio* version of *It's a Wonderful Life* featured James Stewart and Donna Reed recreating their film roles. Handling the additional roles were some very talented radio actors: Victor Moore as Clarence, Leo Cleary as Uncle Billy, Edwin Maxwell as Mr. Potter, Bill Johnstone as Mr. Bailey, John McIntire as Joseph, and Janet Scott as Ma Bailey.

Although most known as a motion picture actor, Jimmy Stewart was no slouch in front of the microphone—in studio solitude or in front of an audience. In the late 1930s

the versatile thespian hosted the Maxwell House show *Good News* and made literally hundreds of guest appearances on such prestigious radio programs like *Hollywood Star Playhouse, The Charlie McCarthy Show, The Jack Benny Program, Suspense, Cavalcade of America,* and *The Screen Director's Playhouse.* In the early 1950s, while juggling a busy film and stage career, he starred in his own radio western series, *The Six Shooter.*

In 1949, *It's a Wonderful Life* was once again adapted for a radio series called *Screen Director's Assignment* (later called *Screen Director's Playhouse*), a program that ran from 1949 to 1951. Frank Capra was the guest "screen director" on this show, aired on May 8, 1949, and Capra could think of no other to perform the role of George than his old pal, Jimmy Stewart. The role of Clarence was perfectly delivered by squeaky voiced Arthur Q. Bryan, most known as the original voice of Elmer Fudd in the Warner Brothers cartoons. (As Clarence, Bryan brought the same cute delivery that he gave Elmer Fudd as he chased that wascawy wabbit, Bugs Bunny.) Barbara Eiler portrayed Mary Hatch and veteran radio artist Hans Conried, known for his impeccable diction, was Mr. Potter. (Remember Conried as Wrongway Feldman on TV's *Gilligan's Island* or Snidely Whiplash on *Dudley Do Right?*) Irene Tedrow portrayed Ma Bailey, Herb Butterfield portrayed Uncle Billy, and Joseph Granby was "Doc" Gower. Granby, by the way, was heard as one of the heavenly voices in the opening of the film version of *It's a Wonderful Life.* (Note: Both radio versions were eventually digitally restored and remastered for release by Radio Spirits, Inc., and today can be found on both cassette and CD.)

❖❖❖❖❖

As part of the publicity for *It's a Wonderful Life,* Jimmy Stewart appeared on the Louella Parsons radio program, a gossipy talk and interview show sponsored by Woodbury soap and cosmetics. His scripted "interview" banter was broadcast in the early evening of January 5, 1947, from Hollywood. This transcript, courtesy of the

Arthur Q. Bryan, the original voice of Elmer Fudd, portrayed Clarence the angel, who helps "a vewwy vewwy twoubled" George Bailey, in the 1949 NBC radio broadcast of It's a Wonderful Life, *starring Jimmy Stewart.*

Louella Parsons Collection at the USC Cinema-Television Library, provides an example as to the fluffy type of promotion common in the day. Parsons, the legendary Hollywood gossip columnist, was presenting *It's a Wonderful Life* an award, plus she could not help but quiz its star about his personal life as well. The show's announcer, Marvin Miller, opened the show:

ANNOUNCER

The Louella Parsons–Woodbury award for the best picture of the month.

PARSONS

The Louella Parsons–Woodbury Award this month goes to Liberty Films' very first picture, *It's a Wonderful Life.* It's a wonderful, heartwarming comedy about a small town man who carries everyone's burdens. He thinks himself a failure and wished he had never been born until his guardian angel shows him what the world would have missed without him. It's Frank Capra at his best and it stars Jimmy Stewart, Donna Reed, and Lionel Barrymore. It's Jimmy's first picture in five years and he's more America's own boy than ever. I am very proud tonight to have Jimmy in his first radio interview since he stepped out of uniform. Welcome home, Jimmy.

STEWART

Thanks, Louella. I'm sure glad to be home.

PARSONS

Jimmy, tell me, do you think the war changed you?

STEWART

Yes. It taught me to be lazy. It really did. I found out laziness is good—if you don't run it into the ground, of course. I used to work all the time—but when I got out of uniform

I didn't do anything for seven wonderful months except go to parties, drink cold tea, and talk big.

PARSONS

Now come on, you never talked big in your life. But tell me, Jimmy, now that you're back, what's on your mind?

STEWART

Nothing. Honestly. I'm not mad at anybody. No, I'm not mad at a soul.

PARSONS

You mean you haven't any axe to grind?

STEWART

Axe to grind? I don't even have an axe.

PARSONS

But Jimmy, you must have some ambition?

STEWART

Well, yes. The thing I've been working up to is I'd like to break 90 at golf. I'm not kidding. It's gotten to be sort of embarrassing.

PARSONS

Ninety? I've never broken a hundred.

STEWART

Then I've got news for you. I haven't broken 100 either and I've been playing golf ever since I got back from the army.

PARSONS

Didn't you play before you went into the service?

STEWART

No, this is the first time. People say to me, "A big skinny fellow like you must be able to hit that little golf ball a mile." That's a very discouraging thing to have said to you.

PARSONS

You mean you can't do that?

STEWART

I mean I definitely can't do that. You remember the other day when it was foggy?

PARSONS

Certainly.

STEWART

Well, I played seven holes that day and lost eight balls.

PARSONS

That must have made the caddy happy.

STEWART

Oh, I lost the caddy, too.

PARSONS

But Jimmy, you look as though you'd be good at sports.

STEWART

You see!

PARSONS

I see we'd better change the subject. So answer me this one. Didn't you dread going back to work?

STEWART

Well, I was worried. I'd been away for five years. I didn't know how much of the knack of acting I'd lost. It is a skill, you know. The first day on *It's a Wonderful Life* I couldn't remember my lines. I couldn't remember my hat size. I still can't. I had to go home and study and study where before I just used to look at the script once and I knew it.

PARSONS

Why did you pick *It's a Wonderful Life* for your return picture?

STEWART

Well, first because Frank Capra was directing it. Frank was just out of service too, and nervous like I was. And then I liked the story because it was about the average guy. There's not enough stories about the average guy.

PARSONS
You know, some actors think average guy parts are dull.

STEWART
They don't have to be. A character who takes dope and beats his grandmother can be dull, too. I think a picture doesn't have to be a striptease act . . . mind you I'm not knocking that . . . to be dramatically effective. I want to be in movies that are something worthwhile for people to see, not just something that they go to between trains.

PARSONS
Well, you certainly achieve your ambition with this picture. *It's a Wonderful Life* is really worthwhile.

STEWART
That's Frank Capra's hope and my hope. It's the kind of thing I want to keep on doing.

PARSONS
That's good news for movie fans, I'll say. Jimmy, I'm about to ask you that inevitable question.

STEWART
Are you?

PARSONS
Doesn't every interviewer always ask you when you're going to get married?

STEWART
Always.

PARSONS
What do you answer?

STEWART
I observe two minutes of respectful silence.

PARSONS
No, Jimmy, we've only got a couple of seconds left.

STEWART
Well, I could say goodbye, Louella, and thanks very much for honoring *It's a Wonderful Life* with your award. It makes me and Frank Capra and Donna Reed and Lionel Barrymore and all the rest of us mighty proud.

PARSONS
But won't you please give me a message for Dan Cupid? Surely there's something you can say.

STEWART
All right. Here it is. When you hear this tone, it's Jimmy Stewart scramming out of here. Goodnight, Louella.

PARSONS
Good night, Jimmy. (Parsons laughs).
Organ
Commercial Theme.

⚮⚮⚮⚮

The most elaborate radio adaptation of *It's a Wonderful Life* was broadcast long after radio dramas fell out of fashion. In December 1997, Jimmy Hawkins (who played the youngest Bailey in the film) produced a live radio presentation re-titled *Merry Christmas, George Bailey*. Presented in front of a live audience, this star-studded radio drama featured one distinct difference: there were television cameras surrounding the lineup of actors. The show was taped for television broadcast on PBS that Christmas night. Even if you watched the performance on television, it was hard not to close your eyes and imagine, if just for a few minutes, that you were listening to an old-fashioned radio show.

The production, performed at the famous Southern California Pasadena Playhouse, benefited the Elizabeth Glaser Pediatric AIDS Foundation, and featured a stellar cast gathered from Hollywood and Broadway: Bill Pullman starred as George, Penelope Ann Miller portrayed Mary, Sally Field performed Ma Bailey, Nathan Lane was an appropriately funny Clarence, Martin Landau was Mr. Potter, Jerry Van Dyke was Uncle Billy, Bronson Pinchot was the bank examiner, and Joe Mantegna read as Joseph in heaven.

The actors stood in front of vintage-style microphones, their pencils in hand for quick notes, and acted from a clever script that had been adapted from the 1947 *Lux Theatre* show as well as the motion picture.

The broadcast also included musical orchestration from Dimitri Tiomkin's original movie score.

Television critic Don Heckman noted in the *L.A. Times*: "Viewed as television, the show initially has an appealingly archaic quality. It's fascinating to watch the differences between the actors as they deal with the relatively unfamiliar technique—for most of them—of acting with only their voices. Predictably, the most effective are those with the most idiosyncratic vocal styles—Lane's quirky, inimitable sound; Jerry Van Dyke playing Uncle Billy in his familiar, wacky, screw-up style; and Carol Kane (as Mary's mother) creating yet another ear-grating but hilarious scold . . . Pullman's romance with Miller has its charming moments, and Landau brings intensity to every line he utters."

Reviews

The reviews weren't always so wonderful. It may be surprising to know, more than half a century later, but reaction to *It's a Wonderful Life*'s debut in late 1946 and early 1947 was not unanimously positive among the critics. At times they found the story to be too much to believe. For the most part, however, all agreed that the film was an amazing piece of cinema art and the actor's performances were top notch in every respect. *It's a Wonderful Life,* on the whole, accrued some marvelous comments from writers across the land. Forget the few snotty critics. It has always been the audience who took this movie home with them in their heart.

The film came out stumbling with a crippled publicity campaign, which may have contributed to the lack of press coverage that otherwise would have heightened its debut. Late in 1946, RKO Studios decided to rush the film to theaters before Christmas rather than after the holidays as scheduled. This caused a mad scramble with the labs to get film prints made and distributed in time to the major cities. The general release date of the film was January 30, 1947; however, the scurry and push before year's end made the film eligible for the 1946 Oscar race, and it made sense to see it as a holiday film. The publicity campaign was already set and there was not much time for changes.

It's hard not to notice the conspicuous lack of holiday images used on the lobby cards, one-sheets, and other printed materials used to promote the film. In *The It's a Wonderful Life Book,* author Jeanine Basinger points out that "the moviegoer got the impression that the movie was a happy-go-lucky warm love story, reminiscent of the screwball comedies of the thirties . . . there was no suggestion of the darker aspects: the word 'suicide' appeared nowhere. No copy spoke of a man confronting a crisis and triumphing over it."

Because of the film's hurried release before the holidays, the film's box office receipts were not up to expectations—even into January. Who knows what would have

In the 1970s and '80s, It's a Wonderful Life *was rediscovered by countless generations, young and old.*

happened if the film had landed in theaters across the country following the holidays? According to Basinger, the country was hit with heavy precipitation and subzero temperatures that December. "Ticket sales in theaters and movie houses hit rock bottom on cold nights, and with the need for last minute Christmas shopping adding to the problem, the film opened 'slow,' causing Capra to have his first real worries about the picture's potential box office success."

However, as everyone now knows, *It's a Wonderful Life* eventually did become a "Christmas film," a holiday classic, a perennial for the American masses—although that was not Capra's original intent. And it was all due to television, not the theater screenings.

Here's what the critics of the day had to say:

While the film as a whole lacks unity and some of the scenes are exaggerated beyond reason, there are touches by Capra and certain performances which warrant your attention. . . . James Stewart has moments of great charm and touching appeal as the harassed young man, but he also overplays the scene of his furious frustration. Much quieter, but thoroughly delightful, is Donna Reed as the girl he finally marries, and Henry Travers gives the whole thing a great lift when he comes on as the guardian angel.

VIRGINIA WRIGHT, LOS ANGELES DAILY NEWS,
DECEMBER 26, 1946

Last night the Globe Theatre presented Broadway moviegoers with their finest Christmas present, a warm and merry comedy called It's a Wonderful Life.

NEW YORK SUN, DECEMBER 21, 1946

Sure, Uncle Billy's ecstatic—he won't be going to jail.

Capra took an idea that appeared in pamphlet form that RKO formerly owned and, together with his writers, developed one of the most refreshing stories that has ever been photographed. . . . The creation of the picture story in itself will probably win every award that can be bestowed on such a work, with each of the artists assigned by Capra fitting their parts so well you could possibly imagine that it was written with that artist in mind, and that goes from the most important to the small bit roles.

W. J. WILKERSON, THE HOLLYWOOD REPORTER,
DECEMBER 11, 1946

Frank Capra is back with a bang. It's a Wonderful Life is an all-American picture—that goes for caliber and its appeal—a picture that is both an enjoyable and enriching entertainment experience.

BOX OFFICE DIGEST, DECEMBER 19, 1946

It's a Wonderful Life is a pretty wonderful movie . . . in unskilled hands, this moral fable might have been dully preachy. Director Capra's inventiveness, humor and affection for human beings keep it glowing with life and excitement. Stewart's warmhearted playing of what might have been a goody-goody role is a constant delight. And if director Capra's Christmas-cheer ending is slightly hoked up to make it richer and happier than life, that is the way many a good fable ends.

TIME, DECEMBER 23, 1946

This is a sentimental, heart-warming, natural story. It's the kind you'll enjoy—so perfect for this Christmas time, so poignant that you'll love it.

None of us dared hope that it would be as good as it is. It's a Wonderful Life is the sort of picture that [Capra] has always done best—a story of simple people. Of course, you might take issue with him, for he always makes the rich people the heavies and the poor people the heroes. All rich people cannot be meanies.

The idea of It's a Wonderful Life is original. If it's corny, I say let's have more corn.

LOUELLA PARSONS, LOS ANGELES EXAMINER,
DECEMBER 20, 1946

A glorious picture for the holiday season. . . . This one has the substance of which great movies are made.

CHICAGO HERALD AMERICAN, DECEMBER 27, 1946

Capra's trick is that he can make it stick without being sticky. Wonderful Life is sentimental, but so expertly written, directed, and acted that you want to believe it. Some of it is unashamed fantasy, but it is fantasy that beguiles rather than bewilders.

There are any number of knowing performances—including those of Beulah Bondi, Ward Bond, Frank Faylen, and Frank Albertson—but the topper is Stewart's adult, appealing, postwar impersonation of the frustrated stay-at-home who learns (to the tune of cash and Christmas carols) that wealth is measured in terms of people he can call friends.

NEWSWEEK, DECEMBER 30, 1946

This couldn't be other than a Capra picture, the humanness of its story the dominant factor at every turn of situation. His discretion of the individual characterizations delivered is also distinctively his, and the performances from the starring roles of James Stewart and Donna Reed down to the smallest bit are magnificent. When Capra is at his best, no one can top him.

JACK GRANT, THE HOLLYWOOD REPORTER, DECEMBER 19, 1946

Except for one overly theatrical stock character, the tight-fisted town banker, the family, friends and neighbors are all cut from durable life-like patterns and director Capra has made their trials and worries so real that women will weep and even blasé patrons will get a lump in their throat. . . .

Only Lionel Barrymore, made up to resemble John L. Lewis and sound like Scrooge, hams up the melodramatic role of the greedy town banker.

Ordinarily James Stewart just has to fall naturally into his easy-going, much

beset-upon hero role to win audiences over to his side, but in this case, he also has some magnificent moments of rage and despair which stamp him as a first-rate actor.

Covering a twenty-year period, the picture is also packed with nostalgic moments and those expert touches in which Capra excels. . . . It's a picture of which the industry can be proud.

FRANK LEYENDECKER, FILM BULLETIN, DECEMBER 23, 1946

Gloria Grahame grabbed everyone's attention as Violet Bick, the tease of Bedford Falls. It's a Wonderful Life swept the honey-haired actress into stardom and put her on the cover of Life magazine in October 1946; and for the first time critics began noticing her acting abilities too.

4

After Life

It's the damnedest thing I've ever seen. This film has a life of its own now, and I can look at it like I had nothing to do with it. I'm like a parent whose kid grows up to be president. I'm proud as hell, but it's the kid who did the work. I didn't even think of it as a Christmas story when I first ran across it. I just liked the idea.

↦FRANK CAPRA, *WALL STREET JOURNAL*, DECEMBER 1984

A funny thing happened with this film: television. Just like the strange case of *The Wizard of Oz*, neither film was propelled into super-popularity until television took hold and put them right in the living rooms of millions of viewers, decade after decade, gathering generation after generation. *The Wizard of Oz* had a head start with viewers, being first broadcast in the 1950s. But let's step back a moment.

When *It's a Wonderful Life* first hit theaters, it was well received by moviegoers and the press. *Life* devoted a nice spread, *Time* gave it a glowing review, and *Newsweek* even put it on their cover. It barely recouped its $2.7 million dollar budget, so financially it fell short. Following a "moderately successful" original release (as some still called it), Capra took his Liberty Films company and began liquidating the property.

At a 1985 luncheon honoring Frank Capra, the eighty-seven-year-old director posed with his long-time friend and film associate, Jimmy Stewart.

In May 1947, he sold everything to Paramount Pictures for under one million dollars, and in making this deal Capra relinquished his rights to *It's a Wonderful Life* and set his baby free. Capra had no idea what was to come.

Eventually the film "became an orphan, passed from one corporate foster parent to another," wrote John McDonough in the *Wall Street Journal*. In the 1950s it was re-released in theaters and finally was acquired by Republic Pictures in 1969.

"Then something incredible happened," McDonough added. "A guardian angel suddenly appeared in the form of television. Slowly stations learned they could show this picture any time they wanted and it wouldn't cost them a cent. And show it they did. Every Christmas millions of new viewers discovered it and came to adore it."

You see, in 1973, *It's a Wonderful Life*, as a legal property, fell into public domain because, due to a clerical error, its copyright lapsed. Television stations across the nation began airing it regularly during the holiday season. This movie became a Christmas chestnut, roasted time and time again. Independent video dealerships began releasing their own versions on VHS, in original black and white and bastardized with icky colorization.

Frank Capra was smiling big—until he saw the colorized version; then he was appalled. "They ruined it," he told reporters, "they splashed it all over with Easter egg colors and they ruined it. *It's a Wonderful Life* was filmed in black and white. The makeup, the sets, the costumes, the camera and the laboratory work were all designed for black and white films, for a black and white palette, not color. It's a different technique. The male actors wore no makeup and the actresses only that which they wore every day. I wanted everyone to look natural. Then came colorization and poured pastels over every-

Enter Clarence Odbody, guardian angel second class, who gives George a vivid look into the world as it might have been if he'd never been born. Mr. Capra draws us into a fantasy nightmare that bores into the deepest rings of earthly hell. The horrors build to a crescendo until George, teetering on the brink of the abyss, pleads to live again. For a few emotionally charged seconds the entire picture seems to stop. Then sprinkles of snow flutter down, and the nightmare is over. But not the movie. During the final 12 minutes Mr. Capra lays climax on top of climax, achieving a breathtaking emotional impact.

⮨JOHN MCDONOUGH

From 1958 to 1966, Donna Stone (Donna Reed) was the ideal TV mom. *Left:* Donna Stone discovers the true spirit of Christmas in this first-season holiday episode of *The Donna Reed Show*, December 24, 1958, on ABC-TV. *Below:* Also in the cast were Shelley Fabares, Carl Betz, and young Paul Petersen.

thing . . . even the villain looks pink and cheerful."

In the mid-1990s, Republic Pictures set out to lasso this old warhorse back into their stable. The studio asserted they owned the underlying rights to the movie and went to the estate of Philip Van Doren Stern and acquired the rights to his short story, "The Greatest Gift," on which the movie is based. While doing so, they also renewed the rights to much of the copyrighted music in the film, reestablishing broadcasting rights for themselves. Exploitation by television stations around the country stopped, but adoration for the holiday story did not.

Since that time, the movie has been beautifully remastered, restored, and released on VHS and DVD with stunning clarity. NBC Television has aired the film in prime time consecutively for nearly ten years, sometimes twice in a holiday season, airing around Thanksgiving and at Christmas.

Those Bailey Kids

In November 1993, atop a special Bedford Falls float in the annual Hollywood Christmas Parade, a special reunion took place: the four Bailey kids, Peter (Larry Simms), Tommy (Jimmy Hawkins), Janie (Carol Coombs Mueller), and Zuzu (Karolyn Grimes), were together again for the first time in almost fifty years, since they had worked for twelve days on the film as a family. More than 750,000 people cheered as the cast members waved and traveled slowly along Sunset Boulevard; people could be heard yelling out "Baileys! Baileys!" and some shouting out "Zuzu!" Some of the

Baileys were in tears, the reception was so mighty.

The four children who played the Bailey kids in It's a Wonderful Life reunited in late 1993 under the auspices of Target Stores, which adopted It's a Wonderful Life for their themed holiday promotion that year. The former child actors, at that time all nearing their sixties, appeared in several states at Christmas events and signed autographs by the thousands. During the tour, their faces were splashed in magazine stories, from People to TV Guide, and newspapers across the country ran articles describing their reunion. While in Los Angeles, they visited Soundstage 14 where the film was made at Culver Studios, and even stopped by Beverly Hills High School's swim gym to see the floor expand with the pool underneath. The tour gave them ample opportunity to catch up with each other's lives and swap stories—including how much each earned during the movie. Larry Simms received $100 a day, the two girls received $75 per day each, and Jimmy Hawkins, little Tommy, got $50 a day. "I guess they paid by the pound," joked Hawkins.

"This tour has been like a miracle," said Karolyn Grimes, who, as little Zuzu, spoke one of the movie's most memorable lines: "Teacher says, every time a bell rings, an angel gets its wings." She's inscribed that line on everything from bells to plastic roses, she says.

"The effect this movie has on people is just astounding," said Simms. Now in his sixties and living a very private life, Simms was reluctant to relive the past and tour with the Wonderful Life gang. Following his work in films (he literally grew up on the silver screen playing Alexander Bumstead, aka "Baby Dumpling," in twenty-six of the popular Blondie films from 1938 to 1950, starring Penny Singleton and Arthur Lake) he left show business for good and didn't look back. "Can you believe, I've never seen It's a Wonderful Life all the way through? I've seen bits and pieces when others were watching. It's just amazing how people love that movie."

Simms may be one of the few people in America who hasn't watched the film during the holiday season, but what does he care? He was there. According to Simms (who retired from films at age fifteen), during the production of Wonderful Life he spent much of his off time talking with the sound technicians on the set and observing how they operated the dials and knobs, asking questions about the cables and equipment. One of the technicians took the time to teach young Simms how to disassemble and assemble a tube radio. Maybe that's why Simms went on to a career in telecommunications and worked a fifteen-year stint at NASA's Jet Propulsion Lab.

"It's quite interesting all the stories people share with you, how they were touched and moved by the film," said Jimmy Hawkins in a Los Angeles Times interview. Hawkins, now in his early sixties, is a writer and producer living in Los Angeles, the only one of the four to have remained in show business. Today, Hawkins is a member of the board of directors of the Donna Reed Foundation, headquartered in her hometown of Dennison, Iowa. Set up by friends and family, the foundation awards more than $50,000 a year in scholarships to students who want to pursue a career in the performing arts. "*It's a Wonderful Life* has made quite an impact on my life," he says. "Because of the three books I've written, I was reunited with cast and crew members of the movie and rekindled what turned out to be some really wonderful friendships. I've been invited to Jimmy Stewart's hometown, Indiana, Pennsylvania, by their tourist bureau, and I sit on the advisory board of the Jimmy Stewart Museum."

For Carol Coombs Mueller, a retired school teacher, the question she most often gets cornered with is whether she can still plunk out "Hark! The Herald Angels Sing" on the piano. "Now that the movie's become so popular, everyone wants me to play it," she told the *Los Angeles Times* in 1993. "And I'm not a lot better than when I was ten."

Coombs says she was hired because she had a similar profile to that of Donna Reed, and is grateful for that. But she was also remembered for her crocodile tears in the tense scene where Jimmy Stewart disrupts the family with his rage. "That was the one thing I could do well . . . cry. It wasn't difficult at all."

Today, the four kids are among the few surviving cast members of the film. Lionel Barrymore died in 1955, H. B. Warner in 1958, Thomas Mitchell in 1962, Gloria Grahame in 1981, Donna Reed in 1986, and Jimmy Stewart in 1997. Three of the four kids worked with Jimmy Stewart and Donna Reed at other times in their career. Simms appeared in *Mr. Smith Goes to Washington* (1939). Hawkins appeared with Stewart in the film *Winchester 73* (1950) and worked with Donna Reed on her television sitcom

playing Shelley Fabares's boyfriend. Mueller played Stewart's daughter a second time in the film *Magic Town,* filmed later that same summer of 1946.

Karolyn Grimes never worked with Stewart again on film, but has the distinction of appearing in another Christmas classic, *The Bishop's Wife* (1947), with Cary Grant, David Niven, and Loretta Young. She departed show business abruptly when she was fifteen, under less fortunate circumstances as the other children. When her father died in a car accident, she suddenly found herself out of the movies and in the midwest, where the courts sent her to live with an uncle and his wife. Disapproving of the whole Hollywood existence, her relatives drew the line and cut off all connection with Tinseltown. Grimes was forced to put that part of her life completely in the past. When she returned to Los Angeles to reunite with the Bailey kids in 1993, it was "heavy stuff" for her.

"That part of my life is pretty gone, because the aunt and uncle I lived with wanted it severed, and then it didn't become important anymore. My life, believe me, has not been the very best." Over the years, Grimes has suffered the death of several immediate family members, but all along, her role as Zuzu has carried her through the hard times, she says. "There've been a lot of adverse things happen in my life, but there are balances out there. And the movie itself has affected my life so much, because I have George Bailey's philosophy once he wakes up—that friendships and caring and loving will carry you through anything. And I believe that."

Right: Janie incessantly plunks the keys which, not even subtly, grates nerves and helps build on the tension. Below: "Pete, Janie, Tommy . . . I could eat you up!"

Saturday Night "Life"

It's a *Wonderful Life*, dramatically speaking, leaves an empty space of discontent in the expectations of its viewers. Tragically, George Bailey never achieves his lifelong goals, never escapes poky Bedford Falls to travel the world like he wanted. At the end of the film, his financial misery is temporarily bandaged, but it's never really cured. Potter is left to continue his ways, and there is no obvious sweet revenge.

One hilarious *Saturday Night Live* sketch from December 1986 fixed all that with the perfect resolution for all of us. Introduced by guest host William Shatner, the memorable comedy climax, starring Dana Carvey as George Bailey and complete with scratchy black-and-white film effect, was aired to cheers and went down in TV history as one of *SNL's* most popular film parodies. It just proved, you give the audience what they want and they'll love you for it.

ᴥᴥᴥᴥ

WILLIAM SHATNER
Ladies and gentlemen, tonight marks an historic, not to say a unique moment in the history of both television and cinema. After a search of nearly than forty years, the fabled lost ending of Frank Capra's 1947 film, It's a Wonderful Life, *has been found. Tonight, for the first time anywhere, Saturday Night Live is proud to present this priceless footage—the fully realized vision of an authentic American genius. So, without further ado, here is the lost ending of* It's a Wonderful Life.

The sketch opens with the ending of *Wonderful Life in the Bailey home, money and presents spilling off the table as George Bailey (Dana Carvey) holds little Zuzu in her jammies and a tearful Mary (Jan Hooks) clutches her grateful husband. The town gathers cheerfully as war hero Harry (Dennis Miller) arrives home and reads the telegram from London. "Stop. Sam Wainwright's office instructed to advance money. Stop. Hee Haw and Merry Christmas!"*

Then a frazzled Uncle Billy (Phil Hartman) runs in and announces that he's remembered what he did with the eight thousand bucks. It's revealed that Mr. Potter recently deposited eight thousand dollars into his account and is responsible for the missing cash. The entire group forms an angry lynch mob and heads over to beat the hell out of the town jerk.

When they find Potter (Jon Lovitz) in his wheelchair and smash their way into his plush office with pick axes and baseball bats, George grabs the old man, pushes him out of his wheelchair and proceeds to kick him senseless.

POTTER
Now you stay where you are, George Bailey, you're in enough trouble already.

GEORGE
You made one mistake Mr. Potter. You double-crossed me and you left me alive.

POTTER
Wait just a second, I'll give you the money back.

GEORGE
I don't want the money back, I want a piece of you, Potter! Why I outta pound you. You think the whole world revolves

around you and your money. Well it doesn't, Mr. Potter. In the whole vast configuration of things, you're nothing but a scurvy little spider!

Following a brutal bashing by George, Potter picks himself up off the floor, revealing that he's not even a cripple. That's when the rest of the group begins beating him with clubs and drop-kicking him. The end.

Oscar, Schmoscar

Every time an Oscar is given out, an agent gets his wings.

↦Kathy Bates

During the 75th annual Academy Awards ceremony in 2003, Oscar winner Kathy Bates stepped up to the podium and wryly introduced a segment of the show about actors whose lives were impacted by the respected gold statue they put on their mantel. Frank Capra possessed three of those statuettes, and most of the main cast members of *It's a Wonderful Life* had at least one of their own. James Stewart, Donna Reed, Lionel Barrymore, Thomas Mitchell, and Gloria Grahame all took home Oscars during their careers. Henry Travers, Beulah Bondi, and H. B. Warner were all nominated for performances at some point in their careers.

It's a Wonderful Life was recognized by the Academy, being nominated in five cate-gories: Best Picture, Best Director, Best Actor (James Stewart), Best Editing, and Best Sound Recording. Unfortunately, the film lassoed none of the statues. Frank Capra was, however, honored with the Foreign Correspondents' Golden Globe Award as Best Director.

In the end, *It's a Wonderful Life* received greater accolades than Hollywood could ever bestow in front of an elite audience of pulled faces and black tuxes. Over time, the film captured the hearts of countless viewers around the globe. Its inspiration to the human spirit is incalculable; and the film has been blessed with a unique immortality all its own, beautifully wrapped and tied with a ribbon to the most cherished holiday of the year. Does it get any better than that?

Karolyn Grimes (holding hands with Cary Grant) and Bobbie Anderson (tallest kid) worked together in another Christmas film involving an angel, The Bishop's Wife.

Calling All Angels

Look for some other memorable angels from the supernatural world of film and television in these selected titles:

MOVIES

Here Comes Mr. Jordan (1941)

A Guy Named Joe (1944)

The Bishop's Wife (1947)

Heavenly Daze (1948) short subject

The Bible: In the Beginning (1966)

Heaven Can Wait (1978)

The Heavenly Kid (1985)

Always (1989)

The Preacher's Wife (1996)

Michael (1996)

Wings of Desire (1988)

Angels in the Outfield (1951, 1994)

City of Angels (1998)

TELEVISION

The Smothers Brothers Show (1965–66; series)

The Littlest Angel (1969; TV special)

It Happened One Christmas (1977; TV movie)

Highway to Heaven (1984–89; series)

Heaven Help Us (1994; series)

Touched By an Angel (1994–2003; series)

Before their controversial variety show of the late 1960s, comedians Tom and Dick Smothers starred in their own sitcom, The Smothers Brothers Show, with Tom (left) as an angel who returns to earth each week to visit his brother.

Young Johnnie Whitaker (of TV's Family Affair fame) starred with Fred Gwynne in a musical Hallmark Hall of Fame special, "The Littlest Angel" in 1969.

AFI's Heroes and Villains

I liked George Bailey as a hero because he was a reluctant hero, he was dragged into heroism. . . . My feeling about Mr. Potter is the only thing he really had any control or joy over in the world anymore was his money. In Lionel Barrymore's performance you really get the sense there was this old guy that was just kind of rotting from the inside out. He was just miserable and he was making everybody else miserable.

↞KATHY BATES

In 2003, the American Film Institute tabulated votes selecting the most popular heroes and villains from the past one hundred years of film and presented the winners in a network prime time television special. *It's a Wonderful Life* scored big with two main characters landing in the Top 10. It simply illustrates the staying power of this timeless film, and it's a testament to the talents of the actors who gave us such intense and memorable performances.

Academy Award–winning actress Jodie Foster shared some insightful comments about the appeal George Bailey has for modern audiences: "Everybody's favorite movie is *It's a Wonderful Life* because we get to see George Bailey making these good, humanistic choices. That's the cursed hero, because he'd like to be a bad guy, he'd have much more pleasure in life. Poor George Bailey never has any money, he never has any security, and yet as he looks through his life, he realizes that the sacrifices were worth something, worth something bigger than that."

HEROES

10. T. E. Lawrence (*Lawrence of Arabia*)
9. George Bailey (*It's a Wonderful Life*)
8. Ellen Ripley (*Alien*)
7. Rocky Balboa (*Rocky*)
6. Clarice Starling (*The Silence of the Lambs*)
5. Will Kane (*High Noon*)
4. Rick Blaine (*Casablanca*)
3. James Bond (*James Bond films*)
2. Indiana Jones (*Raiders of the Lost Ark*)
1. Atticus Finch (*To Kill a Mockingbird*)

VILLAINS

10. The Queen (*Snow White and the Seven Dwarfs*)
9. Regan MacNeil (*The Exorcist*)
8. Phyllis Dietrichson (*Double Indemnity*)
7. Alex Forrest (*Fatal Attraction*)
6. Mr. Potter (*It's a Wonderful Life*)
5. Nurse Ratched (*One Flew Over the Cuckoo's Nest*)
4. Wicked Witch of the West (*The Wizard of Oz*)
3. Darth Vader (*Star Wars*)
2. Norman Bates (*Psycho*)
1. Hannibal Lecter (*The Silence of the Lambs*)

A warped, frustrated old man.

Hee Haw! The Nay-Sayers Have Theirs

"Sure, it's beautifully constructed and acted, and stuffed like a Christmas stocking with touching moments. But it's hardly the 'feel-good' movie it seems to be."

—Noel Holston

Come to grips with it: Not everyone is crazy about this motion picture. For some it's less than wonderful. This may come as a shock to the movie's loyalists—sometimes known as "Lifers." (These movie zealots have also been referred to as "Get a Lifers.")

Why do some critics dismiss Capra's masterpiece as fluff? Are they coldhearted? Oh, there are varying reasons film critics and more than a handful of viewers detest the shamelessly syrupy world of Bedford Falls, a celluloid universe carefully created by Frank Capra. But the director didn't care. He admitted this was his personal and philosophic opus, his pride and joy—a film that summed up what he wanted to say about the fundamental decency of the common man.

When *Wonderful Life* was released in 1946, it pulled in, for the most part, over-whelmingly positive reviews. More than half a century later, this film carries a recyclable sentimentalism like no other in motion picture history; it thrives on an existence all of its own—and along the way, this rebirth has irritated some critics, believe it or not. They despise its following. They are confounded by its intense allure. They would rather strike it from the Christmastime schedules. How dare they?

"There's also a Tinkerbell touch of the supernatural to *It's a Wonderful Life* as an ineffectual angel named Clarence tries to earn his wings by preventing George from cashing in his earthly chips. It makes for an odd mixture of the stark and the jolly." That's how *Vanity Fair* critic James Wolcott reassessed this Christmas classic in December 1986, during the throes of the free reign years—when the film fell into public domain and was repeated countless times in major markets across America. With some viewers it reached the point of overload, and George Bailey was no longer welcome during the holidays.

Wolcott noted that the film attracted a sizeable cult over the years from the repeat viewings on television and "to these TV converts, *It's a Wonderful Life* isn't a riffle of images but a holy text."

The drilling of multiple broadcasts on television in the late 1970s and well into the 1980s bore a hole through and even sur-passed all other American television Christmas traditions. Granted, it played and played until some exhausted folks became weary of this twisted rag of worry named George Bailey. Writer Richard Schickel, who both praises and criticizes the film, wondered aloud in a 1994 *GQ* story how we would ever get through another Christmas season, "another orgy of *It's a Wonderful Life* reruns."

And because of this era of overexpo-sure, Schickel characterized the film as an "accidental triumph" for its filmmaker. "Frank Capra's film sank like Aunt Mabel's fruitcake when it was released in 1946; it got good reviews from all the wrong people, and bad reviews from all the right people, and lost a ton of money. It would have taken its rightful place in whimsy heaven if somebody had bothered to renew its copyright in 1974.

"Repetition permitted the public to 'rediscover' a lost 'masterpiece'—just as if they were elitist twits working for some nastily printed film journal."

The nay-sayers may be taking things a little too seriously, criticizing and tinkering with a film made half a century ago, only now using contemporary tools and a more enlightened mentality. Yes, this film may be an acquired taste, but its sweetness is not easy to reject. There are those who find the film a downer and avoid it completely during the holidays. Some are indifferent about this Christmas tale and can take it or leave it at the snowy doorstep each year. And then, there are those who find great fault and want to offer their contrary thoughts.

Wolcott, in his eloquent *Vanity Fair* piece in 1986, didn't want to suspend belief for a holiday tale. He openly disliked Frank Capra's dark presentation of life and the misery suffered by characters within this story most of all, adding "the truth is that most of *It's a Wonderful Life* is just plumb awful." Wolcott wrote:

> Perhaps what has made *It's a Wonderful Life* such a beloved holiday tradition in recent years is that George Bailey now stands for what we want to believe, and Bedford Falls the home we can't go home to again. *It's a Wonderful Life* is the perfect film for the Reagan era, celebrating the old-fashioned values of

home and hearth that everyone knows deep down have eroded. Its false affirmations—I call them false because they spring not from joy but from anxiety—wouldn't have rung true with viewers had Capra not been sincere. Like Reagan, Capra is a blue-sky optimist who filters out bad news. He seems to have a secret pipeline into people's pining desire for an America of a calendar-art past. But peel away the picturesque snows of Bedford Falls and you have a town as petty and stultifying as any that drove Sinclair Lewis to apoplexy.

So what if these negative remarks are disturbing? Legitimate criticism usually is. It jolts us into crossing the line and pondering the other side's opinion. But for those who share a love of *It's a Wonderful Life,* these negative remarks can also more firmly entrench respect for the film.

For most critics, it has nothing to do with the fact that it's presented in gray tones. (I say glorious black and white.) For quite a good many people, actually, the movie seems like an unlikely, even unpalatable slice of Americana, a melancholy vision that just doesn't hold water. So then why does everyone love this movie?

Call it "Capra-corn," call it what you want, love it or pelt it with snowballs, this film has a power and strength all its own—muscle enough to inspire writers such as Wolcott of *Vanity Fair,* Schickel in *GQ,* and Roger Rosenblatt at *Time* magazine to shake their fist in resistance and offer up their counterpoint.

Michael Sragow, critic at the *Los Angeles Herald-Examiner* in 1979, found it difficult to swallow Frank Capra's "single-minded"

close up

IT'S A WONDERFUL LIFE

Nearly 50 years ago, this classic was released to mixed reviews and mediocre box office. It only airs on TV once this year, but thousands of syndicated airings in previous seasons helped make the 1946 fantasy a holiday staple to some, a seasonal torture to others. See the opposing viewpoints below. (3:00)

'S WONDERFUL *by Ray Stackhouse*

Frank Capra considered this heartwarming classic his best film, even claiming that it was "the greatest film *anybody* ever made" prior to 1946. Maybe that's a stretch, but his uplifting fantasy is one of the most popular movies of all time. It's quintessential "Capra-corn"—sweet, tender and soul-nourishing—about a small-town guy (James Stewart) who finds out what the world would have been like if he'd never been born. It manages to affectingly mix pathos, humor and fantasy. What's more, Capra's message that "no man is a failure who has friends" still resonates.

Stewart and Reed

GET A LIFE *by Donica O'Bradovich*

Enough already! When will people get their fill of this cornball tale? At least this year it's only on TV this one time. What's the holiday appeal of a movie about a depressed guy trapped in his home town, surrounded by ingrates and preyed upon by a cranky old man? This creaky bore is trite, tedious and has too many gauzy closeups of Donna Reed. And darned if those Capraesque plotholes aren't glaring after endless airings! Instead, watch any half-hour sitcom. There will surely be several parodies that make the same point without belaboring it for 129 *slooow* minutes.

---

style, stating that the Oscar-winning director's story lacked genuine emotion in scenes. He called Capra's style "overcalculated," and Sragow was irritated by the fact that the Scrooge in this picture doesn't have a change of heart in the end. Although the west coast critic acknowledged that Capra captured the "agony and frustration . . . with an acuteness and authenticity missing from most of his other films," he disliked the style in which the story was told.

"If the entire movie weren't framed by a discussion among God, St. Joseph, and the seraph about George's earthly life, the angel's entrance would come as a shock," Sragow pointed out. "George's frustrations have been etched in a hepped-up, occasion-ally cute and yet realistic style, when the angel appears, it's as if Mother Goose had come to finish a novel begun by Booth Tarkington, or for that matter, Mark Twain—the homespun angel carries around a copy of *Tom Sawyer*.

"Despite his famous Horatio Alger approach to storytelling, these are the qualities that really distinguish all his movies, even this more heartfelt one. Capra doesn't have a unified vision like John Ford's—he uses his pushy style to sell his content, rather than letting the material unfold naturally, poetically.

"It has been suggested," Sragow continued, "that this *angelus ex machina* shows how desperate Capra's belief in good will is—it takes an angel to sustain it. But I think that Capra, the irrepressible showman, simply wanted to push dramatic conflicts to their most dramatic limits. When the angel shows George Bailey what his town would be like if he'd never been born, it's a nightmare of crassness and cynicism."

Critic Roger Rosenblatt, in a December 2000 *Time* magazine essay, called this tale of redemption "no better than so-so." Although Rosenblatt professed to basically like the popular Christmas story, and confessed it has a near mythic stature during the holidays, he also concluded: "the revelation that George Bailey's world was better off with him in it has none of the social message or the moral urgency of Scrooge's ghost-bed conversion. The angel-wing stuff is silly."

A lack of realism in this movie seems to be the impasse for most outspoken critics. Angels and divine intervention are purely fantasy for some human beings. But for billions of Christians around the globe, a faithful trust in God and divine intervention from saints and angels is their core of existence, their manna to sustain them through life's tribulations.

Critic Schickel wants us to douse our belief in angels at the punch bowl each Christmas, and when Clarence pops out for his appearance, try rather to drink in the raw reality within the film in the shape of Jimmy Stewart's portrayal of a desperate protagonist. If you get past the goofiness of the angels, do a little editing on your own and you can make this into a "pretty good feel-bad movie," he concluded. "And in the process remind yourself that sentimentality is the toy that is always broken by Christmas afternoon, making everybody feel rotten. Realism is the gift that keeps on giving."

His ending, a sort of remedy for the fantasy in this film, is just too sobering for me. I ask you: who goes to the movies for pure realism? I don't. Television provides too much of that.

Marlo Thomas, Cloris Leachman, and Orson Welles starred in the not-so-classic 1977 TV remake It Happened One Christmas. Planned as an annual holiday presentation on ABC, this reworking lacked the charisma of It's a Wonderful Life.

It Happened One Christmas

—— Starring ——

MARLO THOMAS
A Christmas Classic!

KCOP-TV 13 TONIGHT AT 8

... For Auld Lang Syne

Admit it: Most people have no idea what the lyrics are to the old standard "Auld Lang Syne." Maybe the melody is an easy recollection, but the words are hard to remember at best. Even singing along at the joyous ending of *It's a Wonderful Life* usually has one starting with "Should old acquaintance be forgot . . ." then it usually trails off into a hum of garbled nonsense. Who actually knows these words?

If you watch the film closely, little Karolyn Grimes messes up the lyrics in the final scene and Jimmy Stewart smiles as he catches Zuzu trying to cover up. (She's supposed to sing, "We'll take a cup o' kindness yet . . . for auld lang syne.") "I was always

embarrassed about that," says Karolyn Grimes, who winces even today when she watches that scene.

The song is of Scottish origin, translated the title means "old long ago" or "old long then" and even "old long since." It was a smooth Gaelic song of reflection of the past, and of toasting with a drink to memories of days gone by. Originally it was a song of friendship and salutation when it was written (dating back to the 1700s), and it was not intended as a holiday tune at all. Not until Canadian orchestra leader Guy Lombardo began the tradition of featuring this folk song as a standard in his annual New Year's Eve radio broadcasted concerts

Watch when Karolyn Grimes (Zuzu) joins in singing "Auld Lang Syne." Jimmy Stewart catches her messing up the words and chuckles.

During this hectic moment, it's difficult to make out what soft-spoken Mr. Gower declares when he scoops money out of a jar. He says: "I made the rounds of my charge accounts."

in the 1920s (and later for decades on television specials from New York City) did "Auld Lang Syne" became ingrained in the minds of Americans as an anthem of year-end festivities. Somehow, *It's a Wonderful Life* took hold of it and made it a Christmas theme too.

But still . . . who knows the words?

Appendix: The Credits

Frank Capra's
It's A Wonderful Life

An RKO Radio Release
Starring

James Stewart	George Bailey
Donna Reed	Mary Hatch Bailey
Lionel Barrymore	Henry F. Potter
Thomas Mitchell	Uncle Billy
Henry Travers	Clarence Odbody AS2
Beulah Bondi	Ma Bailey
Frank Faylen	Ernie, the cabdriver
Ward Bond	Bert, the cop
Gloria Grahame	Violet Bick
H. B. Warner	Mr. Gower
Todd Karns	Harry Bailey
Samuel S. Hinds	Peter "Pa" Bailey
Mary Treen	Cousin Tillie (Building & Loan phone operator)
Charles Williams	Cousin Eustace (Building & Loan accountant)
Frank Albertson	Sam Wainwright
Virginia Patton	Ruth Dakin Bailey

Additional Cast:

Bobbie Anderson	young George Bailey
Larry Simms	Peter Bailey
Carol Coombs	Janie Bailey
Karolyn Grimes	Zuzu Bailey
Jimmy Hawkins	Tommy Bailey
Sheldon Leonard	Nick, the bartender
Bill Edmonds	Guiseppe Martini
Argentina Brunetti	Mrs. Maria Martini
Lillian Randolph	Annie, the maid
Carl Switzer	Freddie (at school dance)

Charles Lane ....Mr. Reineman, Potter's rent collector
Edward Keane ....Tom (Building & Loan officer)
Ronnie Ralph ....young Sam
Jean Gale...young Mary
Jeanine Anne Roose..young Violet
Danny Mummert...young Marty
Georgie Nokes..young Harry
Sara Edwards...Mrs. Hatch, Mary's mother
Frank Hagney ....Potter's goon
Ray Walker ....Joe Hepner, luggage salesman
Harry Holman..Mr. Partridge, school principal
J. Farrell MacDonald ....owner of house
Harold Landon ....Marty Hatch
Bobby Scott ....Mickey (with Alfalfa at school dance)
Harry Cheshire...Dr. Campbell
Charles Halton ....Mr. Carter, the bank examiner
Ed Fetherston ....Horace, the bank teller
Tom Fadden ....tollhouse attendant
Garry Owen ....sign poster
Stanley Andrews ....Mr. Welch
Marian Carr...Jane Wainwright
Dick Elliott..Man on front porch
Ellen Corby ....Mrs. Davis (at Building & Loan)
Al Bridge ....Sheriff
Almira Sessions ....Miss Lester, Potter's secretary
Cy Schindell..Nick's bouncer
Max Wagner...Nick's cashier
Frank Fenton ....Violet's boyfriend (mustache)
Moroni Olsen ....voice of Franklin, senior angel (heaven)
Joseph Granby ....voice of Joseph, angel (heaven)

Also:

Jean Acker, Ernie Adams, Monya Andre, Sam Ash, Mary Bayless, Beth Belden, Joseph E. Bernard, Buz Buckley, Adriana Caselotti, Lane Chandler, Michael Chapin, Tom Chatterton, Edward Clark, Tom Coleman, Bryn Davis, Lew Davis, Harry Denny, Lila Finn (stunt double for Donna Reed), Sam Flint, Curt Foley, Lee Frederick, Herschel Graham, Carl Eric Hansen, Herbert Heywood, Art Howard, Bert Howard, Eddie Kane, Joseph Kearns, Carl

Kent, Milton Kibbee, Effie Laird, Mike Lally, Ethelreda Leopold, Irene Mack, Wilbur Mack, Charles Meakin, Bert Moorhouse, Philip Morris, Frank O'Connor, Netta Packer, Franklin Parker, Cedric Stevens, Charles Sullivan, Charles C. Wilson

Screenplay by
Frances Goodrich, Albert Hackett, and Frank Capra

Additional scenes by
Jo Swerling

Based on a story by
Philip Van Doren Stern

Produced and Directed by
Frank Capra

Musical Score Written and Directed by
Dimitri Tiomkin

Director of Photography
Joseph Walker, ASC, Joseph Biroc

Special Photographic Effects
Russell A. Cully, ASC

Art Director
Jack Okey

Set Decorations
Emile Kuri

Makeup Supervision
Gordon Bau

Film Editor
William Hornbeck

Sound by Richard Van Hessen, Clem Portman

Costume Designs by Edward Stevenson

Assistant Director
Arthur S. Black

Sound by RCA System

Running Time: 132 minutes

Index

About the Author

Stephen Cox grew up in good ol' St. Louis, left of the Mississippi. He received his degree in journalism and communication arts from Park University in Kansas City, Missouri, in 1988. It was in the mid-1980s, somewhere in that haze of dormitory living, the author discovered *It's a Wonderful Life* on television and it became an instant favorite. Eventually, Cox began writing books about classic television, and went on a search to find the surviving midgets from *The Wizard of Oz*, a most unusual journey that he described in what became an amazingly durable book, still in print after a decade. In the early 1990s, that George Bailey curiosity for travel and adventure in Cox led to relocation on the West Coast. His roots in the Midwest, he says, drew him to this movie, and whenever he visits home and family at Christmastime he still hopes for one thing . . . a healthy blanket of wet, crunchy snow.